Gandhi in Contemporary Times

This volume brings together essays that discuss and contextualise Gandhi's ideas on pluralism, religious identity, non-violence, *satyagraha*, and modernity. It interrogates the epistemic foundations of Gandhian thinking and *weltanschauung*, identifies diverse strands within his arguments, and gives it new meaning in contemporary society.

This book focuses on Gandhi's engagements with religious, political, and social conflicts; his reflections on faith and modernity; and his argumentative dialogues with Mohammad Ali Jinnah and B. R. Ambedkar. It provides critical insights into Gandhi's philosophy and suggests ways of engaging with his ethical and moral ideas in contemporary intellectual and political discourse. Comparing and contrasting Gandhian thought and strategies with contemporary issues and conceptions of religious freedom, conflict resolution, and liberalism, the volume reformulates and reconstitutes his intellectual and political legacy.

This book points to new and possible future directions of research on Gandhian concepts and will be useful for scholars in the fields of political science, Gandhian studies, sociology, and philosophy.

S K Srivastava is a consultant surgeon. Apart from publishing papers in professional medical journals, he has edited *Modern Concepts of Surgery* (1992) and is the author of *Breast Care and Cancer* (1999). He has been a freelance commentator on social, political, and health-related issues for national dailies. His interests include sociology and Gandhian studies. He blogs on a variety of issues. He organizes the VIRAJ Lecture Series at India Habitat Centre New Delhi.

Ashok Vohra is former Professor and Head of the Department of Philosophy, Delhi University. He is also the former director of Gandhi Bhavan and Dean of the Arts Faculty, University of Delhi. He has published a number of books and research papers on wide-ranging philosophical themes including Gandhian thought. He has authored *Wittgenstein's Philosophy of Mind* and translated Ludwig Wittgenstein's *Philosophical Investigations*, *Tractatus Logico Philosophicus*, *On Certainty*, and *Culture and Value* into Hindi.

Gandhi in Contemporary Times

Edited by S K Srivastava
and Ashok Vohra

LONDON AND NEW YORK

First published 2020 by Routledge

2 Park Square, Milton Park, Abingdon, Oxon OX14 4RN
605 Third Avenue, New York, NY 10017

Routledge is an imprint of the Taylor & Francis Group, an informa business

First issued in paperback 2021

Copyright © 2020 selection and editorial matter, S K Srivastava and Ashok Vohra; individual chapters, the contributors

The right of S K Srivastava and Ashok Vohra to be identified as the authors of the editorial material, and of the authors for their individual chapters, has been asserted in accordance with sections 77 and 78 of the Copyright, Designs and Patents Act 1988.

All rights reserved. No part of this book may be reprinted or reproduced or utilised in any form or by any electronic, mechanical, or other means, now known or hereafter invented, including photocopying and recording, or in any information storage or retrieval system, without permission in writing from the publishers.

Notice:
Product or corporate names may be trademarks or registered trademarks, and are used only for identification and explanation without intent to infringe.

Publisher's Note

The publisher has gone to great lengths to ensure the quality of this reprint but points out that some imperfections in the original copies may be apparent.

Epigraph is from Nirmal Verma's, *Dhundh Se Uthati Dhun*. Vani Prakashan 2018, page 180. Translation by the editors.

British Library Cataloguing-in-Publication Data
A catalogue record for this book is available from the British Library

Library of Congress Cataloging-in-Publication Data
A catalog record for this book has been requested

ISBN: 978-0-8153-6606-5 (hbk)
ISBN: 978-1-03-217523-2 (pbk)
DOI: 10.4324/9781003016113

Typeset in Sabon
by Apex CoVantage, LLC

To
VIRAJ
Simplicity, Austerity, Excellence

When I think of Gandhi, what is the first thing that comes to mind? An image of a flame – a sliver of light in the darkness, slender and unwavering, occupying minimal space in the darkness; yet burning, so steadily that one is not even aware that it is burning.

– Nirmal Verma

Contents

	List of contributors	viii
	Preface	x
	Introduction	1
	S K SRIVASTAVA	
1	**Spirituality and plurality of religions: a Gandhian perspective**	5
	MRINAL MIRI	
2	**Mahatma Gandhi and religious freedom**	17
	ARVIND SHARMA	
3	**Religious conflicts: a critique of Gandhian methods**	27
	ASHOK VOHRA	
4	**Interfacing Ambedkar and Gandhi**	40
	VALERIAN RODRIGUES	
5	**Gandhi's imaginations of Muslims**	55
	HILAL AHMED	
6	**Gandhi, Kant and superstition**	72
	APAAR KUMAR	
7	**The technology driven modern world and Gandhi**	85
	ANOOP GEORGE	
8	**Negotiating differences in a Gandhian way: *ahimsa*, love, compassion and the gift of fearlessness**	97
	BINDU PURI	
	Index	110

Contributors

Hilal Ahmed is Associate Professor at the Centre for the Study of Developing Societies, Delhi. His work is on political Islam, Muslim modernities/representation, and politics of symbols in South Asia. His book *Muslim Political Discourse in Postcolonial India: Monuments, Memory, Contestation* (2014) looks at these thematic concerns to make sense of the nature of contemporary Muslim political discourse.

Anoop George received his PhD from IIT Bombay and Master's from the University of Hyderabad. He has been a fellow of Indian Council of Philosophical Research. He taught philosophy at BITS Pilani K. K. Birla Goa campus for more than two years. Currently he is Assistant Professor in the Department of Humanities and Social Sciences at IIT Palakkad. His research interests are continental philosophy, phenomenology, and existentialism with a special focus on modernity, technology, and identity.

Apaar Kumar is Assistant Professor of Philosophy, School of Arts and Sciences, Ahmedabad University, Ahmedabad. He completed his doctoral work in philosophy at Emory University, USA, and he has published in the areas of Kant's metaphysics and epistemology and hermeneutics and phenomenology. His other research interests include issues in ethical and political philosophy. Currently, he is working on Kant's theory of self-consciousness and exploring questions at the interface of philosophical hermeneutics and social ontology.

Mrinal Miri is former Professor of Philosophy and retired Vice Chancellor of North Eastern Hill University, Shillong. He is also a former member of the upper house of the Indian parliament and author of several books in different areas of philosophy.

Bindu Puri is Professor of Philosophy and the chairperson at the Centre for Philosophy, School of Social Sciences, Jawaharlal Nehru University, New Delhi. Her main interests are in areas of political philosophy, moral philosophy, and contemporary Indian philosophy. She has published numerous papers and authored *Gandhi and Moral Life* (2004) and *The Tagore-Gandhi Debate: On Matters of Truth and Untruth* (2015), besides several others related to Kant. She has presented papers in various national and international seminars and conferences.

Valerian Rodrigues was formerly Professor of Political Science at Mangalore University and Jawaharlal Nehru University, New Delhi and National Fellow of the Indian Council of Social Science Research. He was the first Ambedkar Chair at Ambedkar University Delhi. His writings include *The Essential Writings of B. R. Ambedkar* (2002), *The Indian Parliament: A Democracy at Work* (2011), co-authored with B. L. Shankar, and *Speaking for Karnataka* (2018), co-authored with Rajendra Chenni, Nataraj Huliyar, and S. Japhet. He has also edited *Conversations with Ambedkar: 10 Ambedkar Memorial Lectures* (2019).

Arvind Sharma is a former IAS officer. He is Birk's Professor of Comparative Religion in the School of Religious Studies at McGill University in Montreal, Canada. He has taught at the University of Queensland, Sydney and at Northeastern, Temple, Boston, and Harvard Universities. He has published extensively in the fields of comparative religion and Indology. He was instrumental, through three Global Conferences (2006, 2011, 2016), in facilitating the adoption of a Universal Declaration of Human Rights by the World's Religions.

S K Srivastava is a consultant surgeon. Apart from publishing papers in professional medical journals, he has edited *Modern Concepts of Surgery* (1992) and is the author of *Breast Care and Cancer* (1999). He has been a freelance commentator on social, political, and health-related issues for national dailies. His interests include sociology and Gandhian studies. He blogs on a variety of issues. He organizes the VIRAJ Lecture Series at India Habitat Centre New Delhi.

Ashok Vohra is former Professor and Head of the Department of Philosophy, Delhi University. He is also the former director of Gandhi Bhavan and Dean of the Arts Faculty, University of Delhi. He has published a number of books and research papers on wide-ranging philosophical themes including Gandhian thought. He has authored *Wittgenstein's Philosophy of Mind* and translated Ludwig Wittgenstein's *Philosophical Investigations*, *Tractatus Logico Philosophicus*, *On Certainty*, and *Culture and Value* into Hindi.

Preface

The two-day VIRAJ Lecture Series – which is held twice a year, in February and October – commenced in February 2014 at the India Habitat Centre (IHC), New Delhi. In October of the same year, eight short films on Gandhi were screened over the course of two days (courtesy the Films Division, Mumbai). Following a good response to this event, VIRAJ began to organize more lectures around Gandhi and the relevance of his thought in contemporary times. These lectures were delivered by eminent scholars and were well-attended.

The lecture format is in tune with the spirit of VIRAJ: simplicity, austerity, and excellence. VIRAJ is neither a trust nor a non-governmental organization. The invited speakers deliver their lecture on a purely voluntary basis. The lectures themselves are a simple affair: no chairperson, speeches, or bouquets. An interactive session follows the lecture. In essence, the VIRAJ Lecture Series – out of which the essays in this volume have emerged – is organized entirely as a forum for scholarly discussion around issues that are cardinal to Gandhi's thoughts.

Gandhi's ideas transcend professional, regional, caste, religious, and national distinctions in that they can serve anyone as a guide for conduct. This thought formed the underlying motivation for inviting scholars to reflect upon the different aspects of Gandhi's thought in the context of contemporary times. The aim was not to deify Gandhi but to grapple with his views in isolation from the fame and mythology associated with his name. The authors in their own way explore whether Gandhi's ideas are vital enough to resolve some of our lived concerns today. It is true that Gandhi's ideas were marginalized in the name of building a modern nation-state. However, it is equally true that, in the decades post-independence, Gandhi's ideas have remained influential not merely in several resistance movements (one thinks of Baba Amte, Sunderlal Bahuguna, Anna Hazare, et al.), but also in intellectually tackling a whole array of difficult problems like environmental degradation, corruption, sectarian conflict and violence, and socioeconomic injustice. The present volume aims to further this larger project: to remember Gandhi by engaging with his ideas. The hope is that such an engagement will not only contribute to the already

Preface xi

substantial Gandhi scholarship but will also get non-academics interested in Gandhi's views.

Many thanks to the VIRAJ Lecture Series invitees who agreed to contribute a chapter for this volume and to the scholars invited to write specially for it. Mrinal Miri has been kind with his help and support and Y. P. Anand, formerly Director of National Gandhi Museum and Library New Delhi, deserves special mention for reading and commenting on all the chapters with constructive suggestions. Thanks are also due to Raj Liberhan, former Director of the India Habitat Centre, for giving initial support to the VIRAJ Lecture Series. The IHC continues to support this series, and their program desk has been particularly helpful in organizing the lectures.

S K Srivastava
Ashok Vohra

Introduction

S K Srivastava

The underlying principle of truth in *My Experiments with Truth* is one of the most challenging aspects of Mahatma Gandhi's philosophy. Here truth refers neither to propositional truth, nor contrary to what the word 'experiment' might suggest, the truth of scientific theories. Instead, it refers to the truth of what one must live by. The word 'my' is also important, because it suggests that while I must myself engage in these experiments, every adult rational being must similarly engage in the search for the truth by which he or she must live. This implies that ethical life (the values I live by) is one of ever deeper reflection, ceaseless questioning in the dense milieu of one's practical life (*swadharma*). Practical life is an enormous complex of interrelationships between different categories of people (parents, spouses, friends, community members, etc.) as well as engagements in different spheres of life like the religious, the secular, the political, the educational, and so on. It is such a milieu that forms the arena of one's ethical life and one's experiments with the truth of this life; it is the space where the search for the answer to the question 'How should I live?' takes place. Gandhi's own answer to this question of how we should live includes the principle of non-violence, the inseparability of the ethical and the spiritual, the priority of the ethical over the religious, the inescapability of the ethical and the spiritual, fellowship of all religions, and so on. These answers – and others that we might yet discover – can form the necessary guiding principles of how we must live our lives at a particular point of time. However, the fact that one has arrived at such an answer does not prove that it is final. This is because the contingencies of human life are so enormous and so frequently unpredictable that the search for truth, the experimentation, can never stop. Every generation must engage in it afresh. Every generation must find its own *yuga dharma*.

What would it mean then in general to ask the Gandhian question in our time and to seek our own answer to it? More specifically, it can be argued that several problems that Gandhi addressed in *Hind Swaraj* remain unresolved, in some form or the other, in our own time. Rapid growth in technology at the cost of our own skills and craft. Competitive consumerism. Chronic agrarian distress leading to farmer suicides. Growing inequality due to the adoption of neoliberal policies. Shortage of basic resources like

2 S K Srivastava

water, especially potable water. The threat of climate change. The persistence of gender and caste inequalities. The threat that political democracies will degenerate into tyranny. The threat of violent religious conflicts. There is a sense of crisis and loss. The essays put together in this volume, in their own different ways, attempt to address these thorny issues by recovering, extending, or interrogating the Gandhian framework.

Mrinal Miri examines Gandhi's assertions that all religions are one 'at heart', that God and Truth go together, and that the search for Truth/God, is the same as the spiritual search for truth of oneself. Self-knowledge requires special efforts, and the life of morality is inalienably connected with it. The arena of the moral is the arena of our ordinary everyday life, and insofar as the moral requires self-knowledge, the spiritual is contingent on the moral. For Gandhi, morality, religion, and mysticism go together. Gandhi also believed that no faith or religion can claim superiority over another. This is a resolute departure from the view held universally not such a long time ago that a particular religion is superior to all others. Gandhi's view that all religions must be equally respected and that no religion is absolutely perfect heralds new conceptions of plurality of religions and of the proper relationship between them captured in his idea of 'fellowship of religions'.

Arvind Sharma contrasts the Gandhian and modern notions of religious freedom through the lenses of religious identity, secularism, and education. On the modern discourse of religious identity, the idea of conversion is based on an exclusive singular identity and the notion of only one God. Thus, this discourse revolves around the freedom not merely to change our own religion but also to persuade others to convert to our religion. For Gandhi, in contrast, one can adopt another religion to change one's life without having to give up one's existing religion. Giving up a religion to acquire a new one entails religious strife. Further, the state is neutral between religions in modern (negative) secularism, while Gandhi's positive secularism requires that the state actively promote dialogue and cooperation among religions. Finally, going beyond confessional and non-confessional religious education, Gandhi advocated that we should not restrict ourselves to studying one religion and understand religion as it is understood by the believers.

In contrast to Miri and Sharma, Ashok Vohra takes a critical approach, arguing that Gandhian methods are not suited to resolving inter-religious conflicts characterized by orthodoxy and fanaticism. He contends that Gandhi's failure to prevent the Partition demonstrates that his emphasis on dialogue and respect for human rights could not accommodate the feelings of perceived injustices and disparities in the conflicting parties. Referring to the Gandhi–Jinnah interaction, he says while Gandhi did everything possible, he 'failed miserably' in resolving the communal discord. Apparently, the author has not considered that while Gandhi could not prevent the Partition, he did succeed in ensuring that post-Partition India came up as a vibrant secular country with a 'common nationality'.

Introduction 3

Contrary to the popular construal of the relationship between Ambedkar and Gandhi, Valerian Rodrigues explores both the continuities and the discontinuities between these great leaders-cum-thinkers. Gandhi and Ambedkar had 'shared perspectives and concerns' in matters such as those relating to human dignity, gender equality, *swaraj*, scientific approach, religion, and political strategy; however, they held different views on the importance of social realities and interaction in our lives, the role of villages in national democracy, and the value of the 'modern turn'. Rodrigues concludes that there was much in common between them on substantive issues and, in their distinct ways, both affirmed the creative human potential and did not regard the colonial categories as adequate to understand the social needs in India. Rodrigues' essay is a welcome reminder of the need to reflect on the contemporary assumption of the generally adversarial character of the Gandhi–Ambedkar relationship.

The chapter by Hilal Ahmed delves into Gandhi's 'imaginations' of the Muslim. While in the *Hind Swaraj* Gandhi had described Muslims as an inseparable part of the Indian nation, after the 1924 communal riots he even thought of the Muslim as a bully – and the Hindu as a coward. Nevertheless he also began to perceive the Prophet's lived life as a struggle for justice, peace, and equality. Ahmed concludes that while Gandhi recognized the official modes of identifying Muslims on the basis of religion, he also reimagined the concept of the 'Muslim' by exploring the multiple meanings of the Quran and through demystification of the Prophet. This enabled Gandhi, unlike Jinnah, to discover the humane face of the lived Islam.

Apaar Kumar studies similarities between Gandhi and Immanuel Kant on their views of the relationship between morality, faith, superstition, and society. Taking as his starting point Gandhi's statement that the Bihar earthquake of 1934 should be seen as 'divine punishment' for the sin of untouchability, a view that Tagore saw as 'unscientific', he finds the Gandhian and the Kantian arguments as similar but also different. Both seek a middle ground between rationality and religion – Gandhi speaks of a living faith and Kant of a rational faith, both distinguishing faith from superstition. But, while for Kant morality presupposes rational faith grounded in practical reason, Gandhi's living faith rests on instinctive feeling, provided its content is socially beneficial. The author views his analysis as a step towards formulating new insights into the relationship between faith, reason, and superstition that are, at least to some extent, generalisable across cultures.

Anoop George discusses Gandhi's view of the growing impact of modern technology and his deep concern about the degradation of values, morality, and integrity due to its unreflective use. While modern civilization had many achievements, Gandhi also saw it as being aggressive, exploitative, and directionless. Gandhi valued certain aspects of Western modernity like freedom, equality, and the scientific temper but also believed that modern technology would make these ideals impossible to achieve. George also discusses how Gandhian economics, which cannot be decoupled from ethics, was an

4   *S K Srivastava*

attempt to delegitimize an economics based on consumerism in favor of a welfare society. Gandhi thus tries to recover the right approach for modern society that remains as relevant today as in his own time.

Bindu Puri analyzes the compelling implications of the Gandhian conception of *ahimsa* and its continuing relevance in a conflict-ridden society. It meant unilateral obligation to negotiate differences by owning 'kinship' even with the hostile 'others' and implied compassion, love, fearlessness, readiness to forget and forgive, utter humility, selflessness, and resort to *satyagraha*. Gandhi considered *ahimsa* as being the means and truth as being the end. The author concludes that Gandhi's *ahimsa* involves a host of moral dispositions and is an alternative to liberal concept of 'tolerance' (which implies a sense of superiority or condescension) as the best way to negotiate differences and conflicts in the contemporary plural world.

This book hopes to generate fresh interest in Gandhi's thought and the question of how it might contribute to resolving some key contemporary issues. But more importantly, students and general readers will find in these essays, written in an accessible manner, a rewarding source of reflection on crucial socio-economic and religious aspects of life in today's world.

1 Spirituality and plurality of religions[1]

A Gandhian perspective[2]

Mrinal Miri

Gandhi believed with utter resoluteness that 'at heart' all religions are one. One expression of this belief is that for Gandhi the God of one religion is the same as the God of all religions. But this statement must be seen in the light of his other equally resolutely held belief that God is Truth and Truth is God. It then becomes easier to understand why Gandhi should have believed that 'at heart' all religions are one: for it is undeniable that all religions accord supremacy to Truth as opposed to falsehood, however arduous the search for the 'real' Truth might be. In Gandhi's words: 'Denial of God we have known. Denial of Truth we have not known' (Iyer, 1993: 159). Gandhi further believed that this search is a spiritual search for the truth of oneself. Spiritual knowledge of the truth of oneself or of the truth of the self is, at the same time, knowledge of the truth of the real and therefore of the Truth and thus of God. The route to such knowledge is moreover an extremely arduous one.

The view that self-knowledge requires efforts of a special kind, that it is a matter of achievement, implies that the self is not transparently, self-evidently, available to us. Within many religious traditions, the assumption is that the original, unknown or epistemically beclouded self is *given* and stands apart from the physical world with which we human beings are willy-nilly engaged. It is, however, precisely this engagement with the physical world that is the stumbling block to achieving authentic self-knowledge. There are many traditionally prescribed practices aimed at removing this stumbling block: some kinds of meditations, yogic exercises, the idea of a spiritual retreat away from the entanglements of everyday life, performance of various kinds and degrees of austerities and so on.

In her excellent paper 'Love and Attention', Janet Martin Soskice (1992) puts the view of one of the traditional Christian conceptions of the 'the spiritual life' that still enjoys great respectability and reverence as follows:

> For each of us, no doubt, a vision is conjured up by the phrase, 'spiritual life' and for most . . . in our personal lives at least this is an eschatological vision – something to be piously hoped for in the future, but far from our daily lives where, spiritually, we just 'bump along'.'
>
> (Soskice, 1992: 61)

6 Mrinal Miri

In its Catholic Christian form it might involve long periods of quiet, focused reflections, dark churches and dignified liturgies. In its higher reaches it involves time spent in contemplative prayer, guided or solitary retreats and sometimes the painful wrestlings with God so beautifully portrayed by the Metaphysical Poets. Above all it involves solitude and collectedness. It does not involve looking after small children. (Ibid 61) Or take the great Sufi tradition. True self-knowledge, which is also necessarily knowledge of God, involves deliberate 'uprooting' of what we call sensory knowledge and complete rejection of knowledge based on argumentation, scholarship and study. In the Sufi tradition this is called *fana* – annihilation. And it is *fana* that finally leads to *baqua* – permanence in God. The role of music in the movement from *fana* to *baqua* is absolutely crucial (at least in the Chisti tradition). A verse extolling the two is introduced by a *quwwal* (musical performer), then it is highlighted by a prominent master or senior devotee, then it becomes the focus of constant repetition to the point of transforming both consciousness and physical existence and then in some cases the result is a shift from ritual engagement to mortal disengagement. The verse, the music, the mood render the listener/devotee blank to any mood save that of the calling, and the call, once heeded, leads to death. To outsiders, it appears as suicide, but to insiders it is surrender to love. The death of the second major Chisti master, Shaykh Qutbad-din Bakhtiyar Kaki, is attributed to such a verse and music (Ernst and Lawrence, 1994: 16–17). Within the high Hindu Brahmanical tradition as well the spiritual life is frequently seen as demanding complete "detachment" from the life of the world – *samsara* – and being firmly established in this detached consciousness – *sthitaprajna*. Sometimes, the original, detached self, which the life of spirituality endeavours to 'recover', is also called the 'witness' consciousness or self – the self as the disengaged witness to *samsaric* life. One difficulty with such views of the original self and self-knowledge is that if life begins with complete ignorance of this self, then how do we know that the spiritual practices that we devise will lead to its knowledge? Must the story rather not be something like the following: we begin with self-knowledge; somewhere, along the way, we lose it or almost lose it, and then devise ways of recovering it? That is why frequently, within such traditions of spirituality, the language of 'forgetfulness' and 'remembering' has a central significance. There is, therefore, self-knowledge before spirituality, but how do we know that the self-knowledge that the spiritual life generates is the same as the self-knowledge that such a life is directed at achieving? The idea of 'forgetfulness' does not help, because even if we allow that we did forget, how do we now know that we remember correctly?

This may sound like logic chopping, and in a way it is. But a more serious difficulty for me with this view of spirituality is that the disengaged self must also be disengaged from the life of morality, because the arena of the moral life is the mundane world of *samsaric* human relationships. The original self is as disengaged from the life of the virtues and vices as it is from all other

Spirituality and plurality of religions 7

aspects of the ordinary world of sense perception, of desires and emotions. My present self is shaped by the contingencies of my engagement with the world around me – my specific location in it, the language that I learn to wield, which I cannot do except in and through relationships with the other, my memories and the human practices in which I willy-nilly get caught up, e.g., the games that I play, the books that I read, the conversations I have, the life within and outside my family, my professional commitments, my friendships and so on. It is in this arena of the contingencies that the so-called virtues and vices – qualities of character such as honesty, courage, justice, love, generosity, jealousy, greed, cowardice, deceitfulness etc. – come necessarily into play; these qualities of character are the very stuff of the moral life – without them the moral/immoral distinction disappears, and therefore morality itself disappears.

Self-knowledge is crucial to the life of morality. Is my honesty genuine? Is my courage not really a cover for my deep-seated cowardice? Is my generosity not really self-seeking by other means? To seek and find authentic answers to questions such as these is an integral part of the life of morality. Self-deceit and self-ignorance are, as it were, constituent hurdles to the life of the virtues, and the ego is their impeccable ally – the 'big fat ego' (Murdoch, 2001). The overcoming of the ego is a necessary step in the battle against the 'cunning' of self-deceit. The spiritual 'discovery' of the self can be given an intelligible, significant content only if it is seen as the overcoming of the ego that leads to a knowledge of the true springs of our actions of our historically and contingently constituted being. Overcoming of the ego also must mean moral transformation, and it is my contention that moral transformation and spiritual self-discovery are of a piece.

A sense of obligation is a necessary element of human life as it is lived. There are many ways of showing this, but the simplest way would be to draw attention to the fact that humans are necessarily language using beings, and to be able to use language is also to be *obliged* to accept external (public, objective) criteria for the correct and incorrect use of language. On this, philosophers of vastly different persuasions are in almost unqualified agreement. The only philosophers who would disagree are behaviourists who believe in a totally causal account of language. But for them there cannot be any such thing as obligation, human or otherwise: there is only compulsion and necessity.

Given that the sense of obligation is embedded in us, the important question for us is: what is special about *moral obligation*? Or, why should one be moral? The question arises against the background of the fact that one of the most profound predicaments of human life is the difficulty of cultivating the moral motive. The difficulty springs from the fact that to be established in the moral form of life requires what Kierkegaard calls the transformation of our 'whole subjectivity'. To be morally motivated is not just to do the right thing in a given situation but to be settled in a state of mind such that

8 *Mrinal Miri*

the right conduct simply flows from it. One of Wittgenstein's aphorisms in *Culture and Value* runs as follows:

> No one can speak the truth, if he has still not mastered himself. He *cannot speak* it – but not because he is not clever enough yet. The truth can be spoken only by someone who is clearly *at home in* it.
>
> (Wittgenstein, 1980: 35e)

One can achieve such a settled state of mind or a state of being at home only by undertaking an arduous internal journey into the 'springs of action, to root attitudes, thence to their expression in conduct' (Miri, 2003: 98). Such a journey frequently involves the dismantling of whole forms of life before a settled state of moral 'purity' is achieved. This is primarily an epistemic journey – a journey of self-discovery overcoming self-deception, self-knowledge overcoming self-ignorance. And, very importantly, self-discovery is a matter of self-education, although it is sometimes claimed that it is a matter of 'grace'. I shall leave this latter claim aside in the following discussion.

The aim of moral self-education is to overcome the powerful impulses towards self-deception and self-ignorance, which tend always to entrench us in forms of life that are devoid of the moral motive. These impulses are powerful because they emanate from the ego. The first step towards overcoming the ego is to develop a form of attention, a concentration of epistemic energy, which will enable us to counter the benighting force of the ego and, as it were, afford a glimpse beyond the ego into the self. An example of such a form of attention is perhaps aesthetic perception. Kant said about aesthetic perception that it quickens our cognitive faculties and induces much thought. In other words, in aesthetic perception, as Mcghee has pointed out,

> there is a receptivity in which ordinary perceptual experience becomes *perceptiveness* – a perceptiveness which reveals to us, through the concrete object of perception a general truth about reality . . . thus we may see in the fading of a flower impermanence-in-itself, and in the moment of seeing discover an attitude to it.
>
> (Mcghee, 1988: 67)

Kant also said that an aesthetic judgment – judgment of taste – is grounded in a delight in the object that does not owe its origin to any representation of some prior interest that we judge the object to further.[3] Many eyebrows may be raised by the invocation of Kant here. But all that needs to be admitted is the *possibility* of such receptivity and such disinterested delight. When Swaminathan, the powerful Indian painter says, 'I paint because I cannot keep away from it, and it takes me away from myself',[4] he affirms, at least in part, the possibility for himself. In the case of moral perception, the receptivity and attention produces insights into moral truths such as: 'true *ahimsa* (love) drives out all fear', 'non-violence is infinitely superior to violence'

Spirituality and plurality of religions   9

(Gandhi, *eCWMG*,[5] Vol. 21: 133), 'true humility is the other side of true dignity' etc. An important aspect of such insight, such quickening of awareness, is that it bears upon one's experience of the world and thence on one's conduct, so that one acts differently from how one would have done otherwise.

To my mind, spirituality is another name for the kind of attentiveness or sensibility that I have talked about and the concentration and gathering of energy that is associated with it. I would also like to think that at least part of the aim of spiritual practices, e.g., meditation, is to achieve the stability of such attentiveness. I take here the example of Gandhi and consider very briefly the curious notion of 'experiments with truth'.

The truth that Gandhi was concerned with was the truth (the real as opposed to the illusory) of the moral life. He believed that there is an 'interior route' to moral truths just as there is an exterior route to the truths of the natural sciences. His experiments consisted in traversing this interior route until the possibility of the moral life is established. They were, as it were, purificatory exercises, which took him to the roots of the matter to what I have called 'springs of action' resulting in 'transformation of subjectivity' and subsequent pulling down of a form of life and founding another. Gandhi's fasts were an instrument of this experimentation, and there were several occasions in his life – in the early years, while in London, in South Africa and back in India – when dismantling of a form of life and establishing another took place. The journey is far from easy. As Gandhi puts it:

> it may entail continuous suffering and the cultivating of endless patience. Thus, step by step we learn to make friends with all the world: we realise the greatness of God or Truth. Our peace of mind increases in spite of suffering, we become braver and more enterprising . . . our pride melts away, and we become humble . . . the evil within us diminish[es] from day to day.
>
> (Gandhi, *eCWMG*, Vol. 49: 408)

The use of the word 'experiment' is also suggestive of the fact that the moral quest – the traversing of the interior route – is not just a psychological journey but an epistemic one – a journey which yields at once self-knowledge and a knowledge of moral truths, such as the ones I mentioned a little earlier on. To achieve such self-knowledge, such quickening of awareness, is also to attain true freedom, *swaraj* – a state where one's actions flow with utter spontaneity from one's knowledge. Freedom is not the capacity to choose at random between alternative courses of action but to act from an integral moral-epistemic stance.

For Gandhi, as for many others, the religious vision is inseparable from spiritual experience, and the authenticity of the latter is guaranteed by the moral transformation that ensues. Morality, religion and mysticism are of a piece. The crucial difference between the Gandhian vision of spiritual life and some 'received' versions of such a life is that for Gandhi, an active, total

10 *Mrinal Miri*

(that is, with one's entire being) engagement with ordinary life – being 'fully there', imaginatively present to that which concerns us – can be informed by the most profound spirituality; spiritual pursuit does not require disengagement from *samsaric* life. To be spiritual and to be moral is to respond with utter *ahimsa* to what requires our response:

> My countrymen are my nearest neighbours. They have become so helpless, so resourceless, so inert that I must concentrate myself on serving them. If I could persuade myself that I should find Him in a Himalayan cave, I would proceed there immediately. But I know that I cannot find Him apart from humanity.
>
> (Gandhi, *eCWMG*, Vol. 69: 321)

'I do not believe that the spiritual law works on a field of its own. On the contrary, it expresses itself only through the ordinary activities of life' (Gandhi, *eCWMG*, Vol. 32: 373).

Working on the spinning wheel, looking after an injured calf, being engaged in *satyagraha* for a particular end, keeping one's own home clean and tidy – each one of these activities can be touched by a joyous spirituality, a sense of being in touch with the real order of things.

It would be interesting to compare the account of spirituality as knowledge of the self that is rooted in historical contingencies with the modern – rather post-modern – discourse of the politics and knowledge of 'identity', the anti-colonial nationalist discourse of Indian identity, the black movement, feminism, ethnicity, subalternity, the *dalit* movement in India and many others. Self-knowledge is the central concern of these discourses, and the aim of such self-knowledge, as in the case of spirituality, is freedom. But one crucial difference between the idea of freedom that is part of the concept of spirituality and the notion of freedom that is embedded in the various discourses of identity is that, while the latter is also seen as freedom from deception, here the deception has not so much to do with the self-aggrandizing strategies of the ego as with the relationships of power between the dominating other and the dominated self. These discourses are, therefore, necessarily also political discourses.

But, of course, the two discourses are importantly connected. Take, for example, the discourse of feminism. The politics of self-knowledge here can lead – and frequently has led – to a deepening perceptiveness and sensibility within an area of moral darkness created and sustained for centuries by the visible and invisible strategies of the 'will to power'. And it is in such unsuspected corners of darkness that the ego thrives and exercises its powers of self-deception. A community's will to power provides a fertile ground for the cunning of the ego to devise its own schemes of self-deception. In the domain of politics the feminist discourse, with all its internal differences and occasionally serious self-questionings, has been a formidable weapon in the 'game' of power; in the moral domain, it can be a source of spiritual

Spirituality and plurality of religions 11

renewal of the kind that I have talked about. And, of course, for someone like Gandhi, politics is the proper arena of moral agency.

Connected with the politics of self-knowledge that I have just talked about is the question of diversity of cultures and civilizations in the world and the possibility or otherwise of intercultural understanding and knowledge. Cultural diversity and the related diversity of visions, including, of course, diversity of epistemic visions, is an inalienable fact of human life. What, then, about self-knowledge, which we have claimed to be embedded in the idea of spirituality? I do not here wish to go into questions of incommensurability of visions and relativism that have been raised in the recent debate in the West about the issues of diversity. I shall limit myself to making just the following point: although the view that a language embodies a form of life or culture is misleading in many ways, there is an element of truth in it. It is misleading because there are many identifiable cultures in the world, which are naturally multilingual. Take, for instance, the culture of the part of India that I come from: Assam. There are many native languages spoken here – with varying degrees of differences between them. While some of them might, linguistically speaking, be members of a *family* of languages, others may belong to different 'families' altogether. However, it will be a grave mistake to split the culture of Assam up into different cultures along linguistic lines. Multilingualism is a part of this culture: people move from one language to another or from one 'dialect' of a particular language to another with a natural ease that is hardly like a schizophrenic jump from one world to another or from one vision to another. The culture, as it were, includes difference or multiplicity within itself. The element of truth in the idea that language is constitutive of a form of life can be stated as follows: language is a *gift* that, as St Augustine might have said, lights up the world for us. It is a *gift* because of its *givenness*. We cannot set out to invent language, because in order to invent language we must already have a language to invent it in. But every language is a distinct way of lighting up the world. Self-knowledge of the kind that we have talked about is necessarily articulated in language, and every language has built into it the possibility of an articulation specific to it. In a multilingual culture such articulation might take an interestingly variegated form. But even if articulation of self-knowledge is presumed to require singularity of language it will be wildly false to think that this will rule out the possibility of conversations between different articulations and transformations as a result of such conversations. There are traditions of spirituality that are distinct but that can yet talk meaningfully with each other. A most powerful validation of the truth of this is the utter authenticity of the life and thought of Gandhi.

Plurality of religions

Now let me come to Gandhi's views about the proper interrelationship between different religions. Gandhi's views are elaborated as a response to the question that he asks himself: how ought I, as a believing Hindu, treat

12 *Mrinal Miri*

other religions? The question had great practical urgency for Gandhi. India was the home to many religions: Hinduism, Buddhism, Jainism, Sikhism, Islam, Christianity and numerous tribal religions. While different religious communities generally lived in harmony with each other, conflicts – frequently violent – did arise and threatened to destroy the very possibility of a community life that is informed by justice and freedom. Why do such conflicts arise? Frequently, of course, they arise because of extraneous causes, such as economic, political and social disparities of one kind or another, but even in a situation where such disparities do not exist or, at least, are minimized, the possibility of conflict is not ruled out, and the reason for this, therefore, must be sought in the internal features of religions themselves. The most important of such features is that there is a claim of superiority over all other religions built into the basic articulation of some religions. This has the potentiality for generating conflict in three different ways:

1   When two religions claim superiority over each other, this can express itself in conduct meant to establish such claims in conflicting practical terms.
2   Even when a particular religion does not claim superiority over others, it is natural for it not to accept a position of inferiority with regard to the others.
3   There are, of course, cases where an individual or a community owing allegiance to a religion is dissatisfied with the religion and embraces another 'superior' one. This may, at least at the initial stage, cause great spiritual anxiety depending on how firmly rooted the individual or the community was in the original religion.

Gandhi's answer to the question, 'How ought I, as a believing Hindu, treat other religions?' is: 'I must treat all religions with equal respect'. We must, of course, distinguish this answer from the same answer from a relativist or a scientific-liberal outlook about religions. The relativist position is:

1   The truth of a religion and the rightness of its various practices are an internal matter of the religion.
2   The religion cannot therefore be judged in terms of criteria that are external to it.
3   No religion, therefore, can judge another to be either inferior or superior.
4   The only civilized attitude is one of respectful indifference.

Whether or not this conclusion follows from relativist premises is, of course, debatable. In any case, it is clear that, for Gandhi, equal respect for all religions could not have been derived from relativist premises. Of course, Gandhi would readily agree that there are many aspects of a religion that are such that questions of propriety or impropriety, rightness or

Spirituality and plurality of religions   13

wrongness in respect of them are internal to the religion, for example, the use of music in certain rituals in Hinduism or Christianity and its prohibition in Islam. Such aspects of a religion, Gandhi would say, belong to the periphery rather than to the moral-spiritual core, which, for Gandhi, is the same for all religions.

Nor, of course, is equal respect to be derived from a scientific-liberal 'sympathy' for all religions. Such a derivation may consist in taking the following steps:

1   Truth claims made by all religions are scientifically untenable.
2   All religions are profound expressions of human creativity and help man cope with psychological and social predicaments of life; thus, they all have both aesthetic and utilitarian value.
3   All religions, therefore, deserve our respect.

From deserving respect to deserving equal respect will, of course, be another and not so easy step. In any event, it is obvious that, for Gandhi, equal respect could not be based on considerations of this kind: to denude religion of truth (or Truth) is to take the life out of it. As opposed to the relativist and scientific-liberal attitude, Gandhi's argument begins with the assertion that the truth of all religions is the same, although there may be diverse paths to this truth: 'If a man reaches the heart of his own religion, he has reached the heart of others too'.[6]

'Religions are different roads so long as we reach the same goal' (Gandhi, *Hind Swaraj* in *eCWMG*, Vol. 10: 271). 'In reality, there are as many religions as there are individuals' (Ibid 270) Gandhi's assertion is not based on a scholarly, theological understanding of the scriptures of different religions, although scriptures of religions other than his own had a profound effect on him. It, therefore, bypasses the entire theological debate that arose in the West in the nineteenth century and continues till today – the debate inspired by the discovery that there were religions other than Christianity (and perhaps Judaism and Islam), which had a basis in spirituality seemingly quite profound. Gandhi's claim is based quite unashamedly on his conviction that spirituality and morality are inseparable, that to have achieved spirituality is to be established in a form of life whose motivating force is love (*ahimsa*) and justice, that spirituality is what breathes life into our religion and, therefore, that every living religion must have a spiritual-moral core:

> I cannot conceive politics as divorced from religion. Indeed, religion should pervade every one of our actions. Here, religion does not mean sectarianism. It means a belief in ordered moral government of the universe. It is not less, because it is unseen. This religion transcends Hinduism, Islam, Christianity, etc. It does not supersede them. It harmonises them and gives them reality.
>
> (Gandhi, *eCWMG*, Vol. 77: 292)

14   *Mrinal Miri*

But all religions also have what may be called temporal aspects, aspects such as doctrines and dogmas (what Gandhi called 'creed'), rituals, modes of worship, use of symbols, aesthetic articulation, social organization and so on. Such aspects may differ widely from religion to religion and may sometimes even be at variance with the moral-spiritual core of a religion. Gandhi's view was that, while such aspects of a religion are most intimately – even inalienably – connected with it, they are nonetheless historically conditioned and are subject to change, reinterpretation and loss of meaning. Frequently, they stand in need of renewal and even abandonment. A look at the history of major religions will show that Gandhi was most probably right about this. Gandhi's view about such aspects of a religion can be summed up as follows. Since they are the means whereby a particular religion finds its specific articulation, and since frequently a man's sense of identity – sense of oneness and integrity – is profoundly linked with the particular religion to which he belongs, there could be a deep emotional bond between him and these aspects of his religion. As Gandhi says about his being a Hindu:

> I can no more describe my feelings for Hinduism than for my wife. She moves me as no other woman in the world can. Nor that she has no faults. I dare say she has many more than I see myself. But the feeling of indissoluble bond is there. Even so I feel about Hinduism with all its faults and limitations. Nothing elates me so much as the music of the Gita or the Ramayana of Tulsidas, the only two books of Hinduism I may be said to know. I know the vice that is going on today in all the great Hindu shrines. But I love them in spite of their unspeakable failings.
>
> (Gandhi, *eCWMG*, Vol. 24: 374)

It is clear from the passage that what Gandhi would say about such an aspect of a religion is that it may be inadequate in one way or another, may degenerate, may be criticized, reformed, revised and renewed. In Gandhi's words:

> All faiths constitute a revelation of truth, but all are imperfect and liable to error. Reverence for other faiths need not blind us to their faults. We must be keenly alive to the defects of our own faiths also, yet not leave it on that account, but try to overcome those defects.
>
> (Gandhi, *eCWMG*, Vol. 50: 78)

One of Gandhi's great missions in life was to reform and renew many Hindu practices that are either intrinsically unacceptable or have become degenerate. Gandhi also believed that the authenticity and effectiveness of criticism of such aspects of religion can be best ensured if they come from within a religion and spring from a love of the religion. If all religions are capable of leading to the Truth, the aim of such criticism cannot be to persuade the follower of the religion in question to abandon his religion and embrace another but to enable him to find the way through his own religion. Gandhi believed that there is an element of *himsa* (ill will) in the wish that another person should give up his traditional faith and embrace another.

> God has created different faiths just as he has votaries thereof. How can I, even secretly, harbour the thought that my neighbour's faith is inferior to mine and wish that he should give up his faith and embrace mine? As a true and loyal friend, I can only wish and pray that he may live and grow perfect in his own faith. In God's house, there are many mansions and they are equally holy.
>
> (Gandhi, *eCWMG*, Vol. 63: 326)

Conclusion

About the numerous tribal faiths in India, Gandhi is reported to have said: 'I would like to be able to join them in their prayers'. Putting all these thoughts together, the conclusion that we must reach, according to Gandhi, is that the ideal relationship between religions of the world is an 'international fellowship' of all religions. Such a fellowship is a community of fellows, that is, of equals who are bound together in a spirit of ahimsa and inspired by the desire genuinely to understand one another; it does not admit of criticism of the other in order to undermine him. 'Our prayer for the others must not be "Give him the light that Thou has given me" but "give him all the light and truth he needs for his highest development"' (Gandhi, Sabarmati, 1928: 17–19 quoted in Bose, 1948: 313). To be established in such a fellowship is once again to authenticate the life of the spirit, a life permeated by self-knowledge, love and justice. To sum up, in this chapter, I have tried to do the following:

1. Show that modern epistemology is unable to provide a basis for a belief in the reality of values; that attempts at finding such a basis within the framework of modern epistemology do not succeed.
2. Indicate that in Gandhi we have an alternative epistemology – an epistemology that can be termed the epistemology of *ahimsa* or love – one that accounts for the possibility of self-knowledge, which is also, at the same time, knowledge of moral truths.
3. Show that, given the Gandhian epistemic scheme, the ideal relationship between different religions of the world is one of international fellowship.

In the end, it is important to remind oneself that Gandhi was not a scholarly philosopher; he did not articulate his philosophical insights in a systematic, argumentative manner. However, as this chapter may have modestly shown, such a reconstruction is possible, and it might yield surprisingly interesting results.

16 *Mrinal Miri*

Notes

1 The chapter is based on a VIRAJ Lecture delivered on October 8, 2015 at India Habitat Centre New Delhi.
2 Some of the ideas in this chapter have been used in two of my previous publications (*Identity and The Moral Life*, New Delhi, Oxford University Press, 2003; "The Spiritual as the Moral" in A. Raghuramaraju (ed.), *Ramchandra Gandhi: The Man and His Philosophy*, Abingdon, UK, Routledge, 2016).
3 See Kant's *Critique of Judgment*, where the idea of totally non-utilitarian conception of aesthetic appreciation finds a powerful assertion and justification.
4 Personal communication with author.
5 Gandhi, M. K., *Collected Works of Mahatma Gandhi*, electronic edition *(eCWMG)*, available at http://gandhiserve.org/cwmg/cwmg.html. Note that between *Collected Works of Mahatma Gandhi* CWMG 100 Volumes, Ahmedabad, Navajivan publishing, 1955) and electronic edition *(eCWMG)* there are disputed differences of content and different volumes and page numbers.
6 Gandhi in conversation with Millie Polak in 1905 in South Africa, broadcast on a BBC radio programme on 7 May, 2004, available at bbc.co.uk/religion/religions/Hinduism/people/Gandhi_1.shtml.

References

Bose, N. K. (Ed.), 1948, *Selections from Gandhi*, Ahmedabad: Navajivan Publishing.

Ernst, C. W. and B. B. Lawrence, 1994, *Sufi Martyrs of Love*, New York: Palgrave.

Gandhi, Mahatma K., *Collected Works of Mahatma Gandhi*, Vol. 1–98, *electronic edition (eCWMG)*, New Delhi: Ministry of Information and Broadcasting, GoI. Accessible online at http://gandhiserve.org/cwmg/cwmg.html.

Gandhi, Mahatma K. "*Hind Swaraj*", in *Collected Works of Mahatma Gandhi*, Vol. 10, *electronic edition (eCWMG)*, New Delhi: Ministry of Information and Broadcasting, GoI. Accessible online at http://gandhiserve.org/cwmg/cwmg.html, pp. 245–315.

Iyer, Raghavan (Ed.), 1993, *The Essential Writings of Mahatma Gandhi*, New Delhi: Oxford University Press.

Mcghee, Michael (Ed.), 1992, *Philosophy Religion and the Spiritual Life*, Cambridge: Cambridge University Press.

Mcghee, Michael, 1988, "In Praise of Mindfulness." *Religious Studies*, 24(1), 65–89 (doi:10.1017/S0034412500001232).

Miri, Mrinal, 2003, *Identity and the Moral Life*, New Delhi: Oxford University Press.

Murdoch, I., 2001, *The Sovereignty of Good*, London: Routledge.

Soskice, Janet Martin, 1992, "Love and Attention", in Michael Mcghee (Ed.), *Philosophy Religion and the Spiritual Life*, Cambridge: Cambridge University Press, pp. 59–72.

Wittgenstein, Ludwig, 1980, *Culture and Value*, edited by G. H. Von Wright and Peter Winch (Tr.), Oxford: Basil Blackwell.

2 Mahatma Gandhi and religious freedom[1]

Arvind Sharma

Introduction

Religious freedom is a relatively modern term. In that sense, one is not likely to find Mahatma Gandhi's views on religious freedom expressed as such. We will, therefore, have to assess his remarks in contexts that impinge on religious freedom. After taking those remarks into account, one feels that the best way to present Gandhi's views on religious freedom is to contrast them with the regnant modern concept of religious freedom. I shall, therefore, first describe the regnant model of religious freedom and then proceed to contrast it with Gandhian views of it.

The modern concept of religious freedom

The modern concept of religious freedom is best developed by analyzing Article 18 of the Universal Declaration of Human Rights, which was adopted by the United Nations on December 10, 1948, the year Mahatma Gandhi was assassinated. The relevant Article runs as follows:

> Everyone has the right to freedom of thought, conscience and religion; this right includes freedom to change his religion or belief, and freedom, either alone or in community with others, and in public or private, to manifest his religion or belief in teaching, practice, worship, and observance.
>
> (Brownlie, 1994, 25a)

If we analyze this Article, we find that religious freedom under it has the following components: 1) religious freedom includes *freedom of thought* as well as *freedom of conscience* along with that *of religion* – as the three are mentioned in one breath in the opening clause. It also includes *freedom of belief*. This becomes clear from a perusal of the Article as a whole; 2) religious freedom includes *freedom to change one's religion or belief*; and 3) religious freedom includes the right to manifest it in public or private. This clause of the Article reveals that manifestation of religious freedom can take

18   *Arvind Sharma*

two forms: Manifesting one's religion in practice for *oneself* or manifesting one's religion through one's religious *community* in teaching, practice, worship, and observance. This includes manifesting one's religious freedom in such a way as to convert others to one's own religion through teaching, practice, worship, and observance.

This second part of the analysis is not immediately obvious upon reading the Article because *in the West a religion is presumed to be missionary* and this sense of mission has two dimensions: one's own commitment to manifest it in one's own life and one's commitment to share it with others in the form of missionary activity. The main features of the modern concept of religious freedom can therefore be summarized as consisting of 1) the freedom to change one's religion, conscience, thought, or belief; 2) the freedom to manifest it in practice in the form it impinges on one's own life and in the form in which it might impinge on the lives of others (Lindholm, 2004, 42).

As noted earlier, Mahatma Gandhi did not express his thoughts on religious freedom directly. Therefore, in order to understand his views on religious freedom, one must recast the modern concept of religious freedom in terms of the discourse prevalent in Gandhi's time. A crucial concept – current in the time of Gandhi and even today – in the discourse on religious matters is that of 'conversion.' The term 'conversion' is used in two senses in the literature on the subject, namely, *internal conversion* and *external conversion*. Internal conversions refer to the 'conversion experience' that people have when their personal life is changed by a profound spiritual experience, of the kind Paul had on the road to Damascus. External conversion means converting people from another religion to one's own religion. In the rest of this chapter, the term conversion will be used in the latter sense unless specified otherwise.

From this point of view, it could be argued that the bedrock assumption of religious freedom consists of freedom of conversion; that one should be able to change one's religion or belief or thought or conscience as one pleases and be able to ask others to do so. This is clearly stated in Article 18: "This right includes the freedom to change his religion or belief" and further that someone has the right to "manifest his religion or belief in teaching, practice, worship and observance." Conversion, thus, possesses a two-fold connotation here: 1) my right to change my religion and 2) my right to ask someone else to change his or her religion. The first meaning is covered by the first half of the Article and the second by the second half. One could even say that religious freedom consists of *two freedoms*: 1) my freedom to change my religion and 2) my freedom to ask someone else to change his or her religion.

On investigating the matter, one discovers that, while Gandhi seems to have believed in the first concept of religious freedom, he had some reservations when it came to the second. These reservations find their classic expression in a conversation he had with C. F. Andrews. The dialogue is about a person who, despite due consideration and deliberation, arrives at

Mahatma Gandhi and religious freedom   19

the conclusion that his salvation does not lie in the religion he is born in but in becoming a Christian. Conversion to Christianity would give him peace. Even such a person, according to Gandhi, should be advised to adhere to his religion – say, Hinduism – and be a good Hindu. He should not be converted to another religion – say, Christianity. C. F. Andrews, who was a staunch believer in the maxim that followers of all religions would attain salvation and peace, did not agree with Gandhi. He opined that if conversion can change the life of a person then there is no harm in converting her. However, Gandhi argued that a group has the right to change the lives of individual but has no right to change their religion. "They can draw their attention to the best in their respective religions and change their lives by asking them to live according to them." Gandhi took the example of a man, the son of *brahmana* parents, who came to him for advice. This man influenced by C. F. Andrews' book wanted to embrace Christianity. Gandhi

> asked him if he thought that the religion of his forefathers was wrong. He said, "No." Then I said: "Is there any difficulty about your accepting the Bible as one of the great religious books of the world and Christ as one of the great teachers?"

Gandhi said to him that C. F. Andrews had never through his books "asked Indians to take up the Bible and embrace Christianity." Apparently, the Brahman's son had misread Andrews' book. Though Andrews did not endorse late M. Mohamed Ali's assertion that "a believing Mussulman, however bad his life, is better than a good Hindu," Andrews did firmly believe that "if a person really needs a change of faith I should not stand in his way." Gandhi argued,

> But don't you see that you do not even give him a chance? You do not even cross-examine him. Supposing a Christian came to me and said he was captivated by a reading of the *Bhagawata* and so wanted to declare himself a Hindu, I should say to him: "No. What the *Bhagawata* offers the Bible also offers. You have not yet made the attempt to find it out. Make the attempt and be a good Christian." He further argued that "If a person wants to believe in the Bible let him say so, but why should he discard his own religion? This proselytization will mean no peace in the world. Religion is a very personal matter. We should by living the life according to our lights share the best with one another, thus adding to the sum total of human effort to reach God." "Consider," continued Gandhi, "whether you are going to accept the position of mutual toleration or of equality of all religions. My position is that all great religions are fundamentally equal. We must have innate respect for other religions as we have for our own. Mind you, not mutual toleration, but equal respect."

(Gandhi, 1958, 230–232)[2]

20   *Arvind Sharma*

At least three points seem to stand out in this exchange so far as Gandhi's position on religious conversion is concerned. First of all, Gandhi emphasizes that what needs to change is *not one's religion but one's life*. (This raises the question: What if one needed to change one's religion to change one's life, as an untouchable might feel in relation to Hinduism?) The second point pertains to *the relative significance of dogma and praxis in one's moral life*. Gandhi is inclined to ignore dogma and is only concerned with the moral quality of life. (This raises the question: What about religions that insist on dogma as a condition of proper moral life?) The third point pertains to *the nature of conversion*: whether it is substitutive or "additive." That is to say, must one *abandon* one's previous religion in order to accept a new one? Gandhi obviously feels that there is no need to do so. His position allows one to *adopt* another religion without having to give up the earlier one. (This raises the question: What of those religions that insist that conversion to them must involve giving up the previous one?)

On the basis of Gandhi's positions, as articulated in this dialogue, the parenthetical questions could be answered as follows. In answer to the first question, Gandhi would say: One may take to a new religion if that is the only way to improve one's moral life, but it should not entail giving up one's previous religion. In other words, one may adopt the religion, if one must to change one's life, but there is no accompanying need to give up one's existing religion. In answer to the second question, Gandhi would say: Only moral life really matters. Dogma may help in securing it, but ultimately only moral life matters. In answer to the third question, Gandhi would say: If one must give up one's previous religion in order to accept a new one, then this kind of proselytization would entail unending religious strife.

A comparison of the modern and Gandhian concepts of religious freedom

A crucial difference between the modern and Gandhian concept of religious freedom turns on the concept of religion itself. The modern concept of religion is essentially the Western concept of religion, which possesses three features that distinguish it from the way religion is understood in other parts of the world. The standard concept of religion in the West regards religion as something *conclusive*, as something *exclusive*, and as something *separative*. That is to say, Judaism, Christianity, and Islam regard themselves in possession of what, to them, is the final revelation from God to human beings. This is what is meant by *conclusive*. They also believe that only those who follow their religion will be saved (with the possible exception of Judaism). This is what makes them *exclusive*. Finally, they believe that if one wants to join them, then one must separate oneself from one's previous religious affiliation or affiliations. In other words, one cannot be a Jew, a Christian, and a Muslim at the same time, although all the three religions believe in one God. Central to all the three features is the concept of singular religious

Mahatma Gandhi and religious freedom 21

identity: that one can only belong to one religion at a time. As secularism is essentially a development within Christianity, even the secular discourse in the West has accepted the features of religion associated with these three members of the Abrahamic religions, namely, that a religion, to be a religion, has to accept the idea of a singular religious identity.

The contrasts between the modern and Gandhian concepts of religious freedom may now be viewed through the following lenses: 1) religious identity, 2) secularism, 3) conversion, and 4) education.

Modern and Gandhian views: religious identity

The first lens is that of religious identity. The Western model of religious freedom rests on the concept of exclusive religious identities, for only in such a context does conversion from one religion to another become an expression of religious freedom. If multiple religious identities are possible, then the question of conversion fades into the background. The religions of the West – Judaism, Christianity, and Islam – are based on exclusive identities. In this sense, the regnant model could be called the *Western model*. However, prior to the imposition of Western discourse on the major cultural areas of Asia, countries such as India, China, and Japan felt quite at home with the concept and practice of multiple religious identities.

India, of course, has now adopted, at least in terms of the decennial census surveys, the model that equates one person with one religion. This is a Western, specifically British, legacy in the case of India. The situation that existed prior to the Western intervention may be gauged by just crossing the border over to Nepal, where Nepalis are quite happy to identify themselves as both Hindus and Buddhists to this day, probably because Nepal did not come directly under British rule.

In the year 2004, Princeton University Press published an English translation of a book on Hinduism by the German scholar Axel Michaels under the title *Hinduism: Past and Present*. Therein, Axel Michaels reports:

> A Nepali, asked if he was a Hindu or a Buddhist, answered: "Yes." All these answers may be imagined with a typical Indian gesture: the head slightly bent and softly tilted, the eyelids shut, the mouth smiling.
>
> (Michaels, 2004, 6)[3]

Apparently, this experience made quite an impression on the German scholar as he alludes to it again later on, at the end of the following passage:

> Therefore, the views of "there is only one god" and "all gods are one" are not so far from one another in the Hindu religions as has often been held. "Thou shalt not make unto thee any graven image" (Exodus 20:4) can also lead to the conclusion: Thou shalt not make only a single graven image. Hence, there is not one single word for god in Sanskrit, but

22 *Arvind Sharma*

many: *īsa/īśvara* ("ruler"), *bhagavat* ("elevated"), *prabhu* ("mighty"), *deva* ("god"), among others; the poet-saint Kabīr uses eighty-six terms for "god". . . .

The consequences of this notion of god are tangible in popular religiosity all over. To use an example I have already cited (Chapter 1), if a Newar in Nepal is asked if he is a Hindu or Buddhist, he might simply answer "yes." To restrict oneself to one position, one god, would be a stingy perspective of divinity for him: He can worship both Buddha and Śiva without getting into a conflict of belief.

(Ibid, 211)

The situation in China is discussed by Julia Ching, who points out "that an important difference between East Asian religious life . . . and the West is that its various communities are not completely separate." She goes on to say: "At issue is the inseparability of religion and culture in East Asia, as well as the syncretism or combination that characterizes all the major religions there" (Ibid). She states finally:

We should make our position clear. There is ground for confusion, we grant, because of the close ties between religion and culture. It is not easy to separate religion and culture in our discussions. This does not mean, however, that the East Asian civilizations are areligious. Some people dismiss customs and rituals as superstitious. But others in the same culture see them as practical means of securing benefit in life. We should be aware that definitions of these traditions in the region are fluid, compared with the roles of religions of West Asian origin, like Christianity or Islam. Moreover, we think that the word 'religion' need not be defined in exclusivist terms, in theistic terms, or even in doctrinal terms.

(Ibid, 319)

The most dramatic illustration of multiple – or at least dual – religious affiliation comes from Japan. Its religious census appears as follows for the year 1985 (see Table 2.1).

Table 2.1

Buddhist	92,000,000 persons	76% of population
Shinto	115,000,000 persons	95% of population
Christian	1,000,000 persons	
New religions	14,000,000 persons	
Total	**223,000,000 persons**	

Source: Ian Reader, *Religion in Contemporary Japan*, p. 6

Mahatma Gandhi and religious freedom 23

The total population of Japan in 1985 was 121,000,000.

Thus, the Western model presupposes exclusive religious identity, while the Gandhian model presupposes multiple religious identity. It is worth noting in this context that many people in the West these days *nominally* belong to one religion or denomination but *functionally* draw freely from other religious traditions as well.

Modern and Gandhian views: secularism

This second lens is that of secularism. Here, one needs to distinguish between *neutral secularism*, *negative secularism*, and *positive secularism*. In the first case, the state is genuinely neutral in relation to religion, which it neither favors nor frowns on. The First Amendment of the U.S. Constitution, which contains both a disestablishment clause and a free-exercise clause, is a good illustration of this position. "Negative secularism" characterized the erstwhile Communist states, which looked upon religion as a negative force in human affairs and promoted atheism. "Positive secularism" would represent a case where the state actively promoted dialogue and co-operation among religions.

The Western model favors neutral secularism; the Gandhian model seems more consistent with what has been just described as positive secularism, especially as he believed in ethical and non-denominational religious instruction (Gandhi, 1958, 261).

Modern and Gandhian views: conversion

The third lens is that of conversion, and the contrast between the Western and the Gandhian positions on this point came out in bold relief in the dialogue between C. F. Andrews and Mahatma Gandhi. The difference between the two positions may be expressed in terms of a distinction drawn by T. M. P. Mahadevan between horizontal and vertical conversion when he says: "real conversion is vertical – i.e. from the lower to the higher concept of God, and not horizontal – i.e. from one formal faith to another" (Mahadevan, 1971, 20).[4] If we extend the concept of vertical conversion to include not merely a higher conception of God but a movement to a higher moral and spiritual level compared to where we are, then the Western model may be said to stand for horizontal conversion and the Gandhian model for vertical.

Modern and Gandhian views: education

Religious education in modern times is basically of two kinds: *confessional* and *non-confessional* (or academic).

By confessional study of religion, we mean the study of religion as it is carried out in a *yeshiva*, a *seminary*, or a *madrasa*. This is the kind of study that the believers carry out regarding their own religion. It is worth reminding

24   Arvind Sharma

ourselves here that all the three Abrahamic religions mentioned earlier, as well as all the so-called world religions such as Hinduism, Buddhism, Jainism, Sikhism, Confucianism, Daoism, Shinto, and so on have their own, often centuries old tradition of studying their own scriptures, doctrines, and practices. The non-confessional study of religion differs from the confessional study of religion in as much as the student of the non-confessional or academic study of religion need not be a believer in any religion. However, the fact that one believes in a religion does not prevent one from carrying out the academic study of religion. The academic study of religion does not require one to be either a believer or a non-believer. In fact, it can be quite reductionistic, that is, it might consider the essence of religion as non-religious, as psychological or sociological, or even political. The study of religion, as it is carried out in modern times, broadly falls into these two categories.

Gandhi's views on the study of religion as part of one's exercise of religious freedom accepts both the modes of studying religion – confessional as well as non-confessional – but also differs from both. It differs from the confessional study of religion in as much as Gandhi would not like such studies to be restricted to that of only one religion, which is often the case with the confessional study of religion. On the other hand, he would also not support the non-confessional, academic study of religion if it becomes reductionistic. Interestingly, his approach comes very close to what is known as the "phenomenological study of religion." The phenomenological study of religion emphasizes the fact that one must understand a religion as it is understood by the believers. Gandhi would approve of this but would also like one's study to enrich one's own moral and spiritual life, which is not a concern of the phenomenology of religion as a method in the study of religion. This point becomes quite clear in the following statement of Mahatma Gandhi:

> I hold that it is the duty of every cultured man or woman to read *sympathetically* the scriptures of the world. If we are to respect others' religions as we would have them to respect our own, a *friendly* study of the world's religions is a sacred duty. We need not dread, upon our grown-up children, the influence of scriptures other than our own. We liberalize their outlook upon life by encouraging them to study freely all that is clean. Fear there would be when someone reads his own scriptures to young people with the intention secretly or openly to converting them. He must then be biased in favor of his own scriptures. For myself, I regard my study of and reverence for the Bible, the Quran, and the other scriptures to be wholly consistent with my claim to be a staunch *Sanatani* Hindu. He is no *Sanatani* Hindu who is narrow, bigoted, and considers evil to be good if it has the sanction of antiquity and it to be found supported in any Sanskrit book. I claim to be a staunch *Sanatani* Hindu because, though I reject all that offends my moral sense, I find the

Mahatma Gandhi and religious freedom 25

Hindu scriptures to satisfy the needs of the soul. My *respectful* study of other religions has not abated my reverence for, or my faith in, the Hindu scriptures. They have indeed left their deep mark upon my understanding of the Hindu scriptures. They have broadened my view of life. They have enabled me to understand more clearly many obscure passages in the Hindu scriptures.

(Gandhi, 1958, 237, emphasis added)

Conclusion

It is time to bring matters to a close. It should be clear from what I have said that the way Mahatma Gandhi engaged religious freedom presents a sharp contrast to the prevailing regnant model of it. According to the concept of religious freedom current in *the West*, the right to religious freedom includes *both* the right to change one's own religion as well as the right, on our part, to ask someone else to change his or her religion. According to Mahatma Gandhi, the exercise of the second freedom compromises someone else's freedom of religion. Mahatma Gandhi believed that proselytization – the practice of asking someone else to change their religion – is a recipe for religious strife. Therefore, for Gandhi, only the first right – the right to change one's religion – truly defines religious freedom, and *not the second*. Mahatma Gandhi's view has its roots in Asian and primal religions and cultures and should perhaps be taken seriously as a corrective to the view of religious freedom current in the West (Bagchi, 2008, 133).

Notes

1 The chapter is based on a VIRAJ Lecture delivered on February 13, 2016 at India Habitat Centre, New Delhi.
2 For the complete C. F. Andrews and Gandhi dialogue see Mahatma Gandhi, *Hindu Dharma*, Ahmedabad: Navjeevan Publishing House, 1950.
3 For a detailed discussion see Alex Micheal, *Hinduism Past and Present*, Princeton and Oxford: Princeton University Press, 2004.
4 T. M. P. Mahadevan has highlighted this in his *Outline of Hinduism*, Bombay: Chetna Ltd., 1971.

References

Bagchi, Reeta. 2008. "Scope for Interfaith Dialogue in Gandhian Thought," *Gandhi Marg* 34, no. 1, p. 133.
Brownlie, Ian (Ed.). 1994. *Basic Documents on Human Rights*. (3rd ed.). Oxford: Clarendon Press, p. 25.
Ching, Julia. 2002. "East Asian Religions," in Willard G. Oxtoby (Ed.), *World Religions: Eastern Traditions*. (2nd ed). Toronto: Oxford University Press, pp. 318, 319.
Gandhi, Mahatma. 1958. *Hindu Dharma*. Ahmedabad: Navajivan Publishing House, pp. 230–232, 237, 261.

26 *Arvind Sharma*

Lindholm, Tore. 2004. "Philosophical and Religious Justifications of Freedom of Religion or Belief," in Tore Lindholm, W. Cole Durham Jr., and Bahia G. Tahzib-Lie, (Eds.), *Facilitating Freedom of Religion or Belief: A Deskbook*. Leiden: Martinus Nijhoff Publications, p. 42.

Mahadevan, T.M.P. 1971. *Outlines of Hinduism*. Bombay: Chetana Limited, p. 20.

Michaels, Axel. 2004. *Hinduism: Past and Present*, trans. Barbara Harshav. Princeton and Oxford: Princeton University Press, pp. 6, 211.

Reader, Ian. 1991. *Religion in Contemporary Japan*. London: Macmillan.

3 Religious conflicts
A critique of Gandhian methods[1]

Ashok Vohra

Understanding the meaning of the terms 'religion' and 'conflict' is key to understanding what 'religious conflict' means in modern society. Gandhi did not use the term conflict, but of all the explanations of the term conflict the most appropriate in his context would be that it is 'an active disagreement between people with opposing opinions or principles'. Gandhi was aware of the difficulties in defining the term religion, therefore, he took pains to explain it in a number of his writings spanning over several years. He was aware that the term religion can be – and is – used in two senses. In the first sense it is used to refer to a sect or an organised religion, and in the second sense it is used to refer to an ethical or moral practice that is rooted in a specific ontology and metaphysics. Besides these the term religion may be used in several other senses, but in whatever sense we may use it, Gandhi firmly believed that 'Religion binds man to God and man to man' (Gandhi, *The Collected Works*, Vol. 78, p. 44). According to him, true religion is that 'which the wise and the good and those who are ever free from passion and hate follow and which appeals to the heart' (Gandhi, *The Collected Works*, Vol. 82, p. 82).

In fact, he himself uses the term in both the senses mentioned earlier. In *Hind Swaraj* (Parel, 2009) he says, 'religion is dear to me. . . . Here I am not thinking of the Hindu, the Mahomedan, or the Zoroastrian religion, but of that religion which underlies all religions' (Gandhi, 1909, p. 36). That Gandhi does not use the term religion to connote such individual religions or faiths is clear when he says, 'By religion, I do not mean formal religion, or customary religion, but that religion which underlies all religions, which brings us face to face with our Maker' (quoted in Prabhu and Rao, 1967, p. 64). Elaborating his use of the term 'religion' further, he says, 'religion does not mean sectarianism. It means a belief in ordered moral government of the universe' (quoted in Krishna Kriplani, 1960, p. 77). This religion, according to him, is that 'which transcends' the limits of any particular religion. It does not supersede individual religions like Hinduism, Islam, Christianity, etc. but 'harmonises them and gives them reality' (quoted in Krishna Kriplani, 1960, p. 77). This kind of religion is one

> which changes one's very nature, which binds one indissolubly to the truth within and whichever purifies. It is permanent element in human

28 *Ashok Vohra*

nature which counts no cost too great in order to find full expression and which leaves the soul utterly restless until it has found itself, known its Maker and appreciated the true correspondence between the Maker and itself.

(quoted in Krishna Kriplani,1960, p. 64)[2]

That Gandhi does not regard religion or being religious or following a religious order or creed as something external, some kind of a 'job' or 'profession' is abundantly clear when he categorically asserts that, 'I do not conceive religion as one of the many activities of mankind'. The main reason for this is that 'the same activity may be governed by the spirit either of religion or of irreligion'. On the contrary he regards being religious as something inherent to humankind. The term religion as used by him pervades in all our activities. Therefore, he concludes, 'For me every, tiniest, activity is governed by what I consider to be my religion' (Mahadev Desai, 1960). He very explicitly admits this fact when he says, 'This is the maxim of life which I have accepted, namely, that no work done by any man, no matter how great he is, will really prosper unless he has a religious backing' (G.A. Natesan, 1933, pp. 377–378).

I would like to call the earlier notion of religion 'metaphysical or the ideal sense'. If one takes religion in the earlier sense then there can be no conflict because it assumes that there is just one universal religion. If this were true, the word religion would then be always used in singular and never in the plural. However, the word religion admits of a plural. Though the import of the prayers recited at Gandhi's meetings were selections from different religions, their purport was the same viz. there is just one God called by different names. He always maintained, 'there is only one God or Allah in every religion. We should thus not hate followers of others religions' (Gandhi, *The Collected Work, Vol. 90*, p. 214). Gandhi himself uses the term in the plural. From his use of 'religions' instead of 'religion' it follows that he was not always using the term in the philosophical or metaphysical or ideal sense explicated earlier. In fact, Gandhi admits that' 'I do not see a time when there would be only one religion on earth in practice'. Giving a rationale for there being a multiplicity of religions he goes on to say, 'In theory, since there is one God, there can only be one religion. But in practice, no two persons I have known have had the same identical conception of God'. From this he concludes, 'there will, perhaps, always be different religions answering to different temperatures and climatic conditions' (quoted in Krishna Kriplani, 1960, p. 79).

We can talk about consensus or conflict, harmony and discord among religions only if there is more than one of the kind. Since the conflict in religions and their followers is a fact of our existence, which was experienced by Gandhi so often, not just in the social but in the political arena also, it would not be wrong to conclude that Gandhi defined 'religion' not just in the earlier metaphysical sense. That Gandhi did not do so is clear from

Religious conflicts 29

the distinction that he made between the terms religion, sect, and faith.[3] These terms because of the ambiguity in their use are very often used interchangeably. Gandhi quite often uses them synonymously. For example, he says, 'God has created different faiths just as He has the votaries thereof' (quoted in Krishna Kriplani, 1960, p. 78). Likewise, he says, 'in reality there are as many religions as there are individuals'. Gandhi further says, 'great religions of the world are . . . all God-given' (quoted in Krishna Kriplani, 1960, p. 78). He believes in the necessity of all the religions at least for 'the people to whom these religions were revealed' (quoted in Krishna Kriplani, 1960, p. 79).

One has the freedom, if one likes, to choose one's religion. Hinduism, of course, is an exception. One cannot choose to be a Hindu; one can only be born a Hindu. According to Gandhi,

> Hinduism does not invite persons of other faiths to join its fold; it enjoins all to follow their own religions.[4] Sister Nivedita, for instance, embraced Hinduism but we do not think of her as a Hindu, nor do we boycott or slight her in any way. There is no question of anybody embracing Hinduism. Everybody can practise Hinduism.
>
> (Gandhi, *The Collected Works*, Vol. 21, p. 315)

The moment one admits the existence of several religions and the condition of its 'necessity' for each of these religions' followers, one has to agree to the implied fact that one has to concede the principle of singular religious adherence. This principle of adherence to just one and only one of the several religions either by birth or by choice is implicit in this conception of religion. In other words, it is not possible to be a follower of the religions of Judaism, Christianity, or Islam, for instance, *at the same time*. This sense of exclusive belonging or singular adherence to a faith is a very important definitional marker of the concept of religion. This 'necessity' and exclusive adherence to one's religion is the cause of strife between the followers of one religion and the other, so much so that it is not just the cause of inter-religious conflicts but also intra-religious conflicts. In Hinduism, they lead to the conflict between the Shaivites and Vaishnavites, between the Shaivas and the Shaktas, and so on. These open and varied differences between one sect and the other led Alberuni to say 'The Hindus differ among themselves', not only about the nature or definition of action or agent alone but also about the nature of God, Brahman and *maya*, relationship between God and man, nature of salvation (*mukti*), nature of soul (*atman*), method of worship, nature of freedom, and the relationship between word and meaning (Alberuni, 1910, p. 30). In fact, there is not one thing that one Hindu says that is not denied by another; there is no universal agreement in their philosophy and their practices.[5] Much more pronounced and violent are the conflicts between the Catholics and the Protestants, between the Shias and the Sunnis, band between Orthodox

30   *Ashok Vohra*

and Conservative Judaism on the one hand and Reform and Reconstructionist Judaism on the other.[6]

Taking the analogy of a tree, Gandhi says,

> The various religions were like the leaves on a tree. No two leaves were alike, yet there was no antagonism between the branches on which they grew. Even so, there is an underlying unity in the variety which we see in God's creation.
>
> (Gandhi, *The Collected Works*, Vol. 21, p. 315)

However, Gandhi laments,

> it was a travesty of true religion to consider one's own religion as superior and other's as inferior. All religions enjoined worship of the one God who was all pervasive. He was present even in a droplet of water or in a tiny speck of dust.
>
> (Gandhi, *The Collected Works*, Vol. 90, p. 402)

However, he himself could not escape the 'psychological necessity' and the natural psychological feeling of 'exclusivism' and 'superiority' for what one considers as 'one's own' – 'mine', as opposed to what belongs to the others. This psychological compulsion makes even a realised and noble soul like Gandhi admit 'I hold for my own religion'; 'I hold my own religion dearer than my country and that, therefore, I am a Hindu first and a nationalist after' (quoted in Prabhu and Rao, 1967, p. 93). This pride in his own religion was to remain with him throughout his life. He time and again asserted,

> I have been born a Hindu and I shall die a Hindu, a *sanātanist* Hindu. If there is salvation for me, it must be as a Hindu. Hinduism absorbs the best in other religions, and there is scope for expansion in it.
>
> (Gandhi, *The Collected Works*, Vol. 93, p. 114)

From this it naturally follows that in Gandhi's opinion Hinduism is superior to other religions because it accumulates the best in every religion and abandons all that is sullied. Even in the matter of prayer he said,

> My Hinduism tells me that along with the Hindu prayer I should also offer the Muslim prayer and the Parsi and Christian prayers. True Hinduism lies in offering prayers of all religions because only he is a good Hindu who is also a good Muslim and a good Parsi.
>
> (Gandhi, *The Collected Works*, Vol. 94, p. 213)

This usage of 'my' and 'your' arouses in us a sense of difference and diffidence, even the sense of superiority and inferiority. For what is mine is much dearer to me than what is yours. I see non-existent good qualities in what is mine and am blind to its defects and shortcomings. Likewise, I am most likely to see non-existent defects in what is yours or others' religion in particular – and possessions in general – and turn a blind eye to what is good in it. This natural psychological commitment to and love for that which is one's own and natural psychological disdain for all that belongs to you or the others, not to speak of small men, leads even one like Gandhi to say, 'I swear by my religion. I will die for it' (quoted in Krishan Kriplani, 1960, p. 103). It is natural for one to take pride and consider his own religion – in which he is born or which he has voluntarily adopted – to be superior to the others and find its rituals, its teachings, its scriptures, its prophets, its founders much more profound and satisfying than all the others. However, 'if a man reaches the heart of his own religion, he has reached the hearts of the others too' (quoted in Krishna Kriplani, 1960, p. 77). A deep understanding of one's own religion makes him realise that 'religions are different roads converging to the same point. What does it matter that we take different roads, so long as we reach the same goal?' (quoted in Krishna Kriplani, 1960, p. 77). A critical and exhaustive grasp of the import of the nature of religions also makes one conclude like Gandhi, '(1) that all religions are true; (2) all religions have some errors in them' (quoted in Krishan Kriplani, 1960, p. 78).[7]

One's own religion and its rites and practices, however irrational they might be for an objective observer, are likely to give one more solace than those of the other religions, however rational they may seem to the neutral, impartial observer. So much so that the practitioner of a religion, in Gandhi's words, admits 'no religion higher than his and the day he would think so he would change his religion' (Gandhi, *The Collected Works*, Vol. 21, p. 49). Though Gandhi repeatedly reminds the followers of different religions 'of the folly of looking upon one religion as better than the other' (U.R. Rao, 1994, p. 39), what to talk of a common practitioner of religion, even great men like Mahatma Gandhi are not able to escape the emotional tendency of considering the religion practised by him as superior. Talking about Hinduism, Gandhi said, 'Hinduism . . . to me is the most glorious religions in the world'. He goes on to say, '(Hinduism), I certainly prize above all other religions'. Talking about his preference for the Hindu religion and its scriptures over other religions he says,

> I am unable to satisfy myself with Orthodox Christianity . . . Hinduism as I know it entirely satisfies my soul, fills my whole being and I find a solace in *Bhagvadgita* and Upanishads that I miss even in the Sermon on the Mount.

About religion one is born in or practices one has adhered to since birth he asks, 'If I tell you to give up your religion, will you do so?' and answers it by saying 'Never' (U.R. Rao, 1994, p. 328). He goes on to recommend, 'Every one of them should remain firm to their religion' (U.R. Rao, 1994, p. 52). Gandhi not only prescribes that everyone must understand his religion and its

32   *Ashok Vohra*

practices 'and remain faithful to her own religion' (U.R. Rao, 1994, p. 26); Gandhi also considers it natural that the follower of a religion should have a 'feeling of sympathy for co-religionists as a natural feeling and common to all nations' (U.R. Rao, 1994, p. 31). That is why he argues, 'If a Hindu wishes to protect his religion, let him do that' (U.R. Rao, 1994, p. 291). At the same time, he criticises the English by saying, 'the English have hopelessly failed to realize the first principle of religion, namely, brotherhood of man' (U.R. Rao, 1994, p. 1). In a letter to the Duke of Connaught he very patronisingly says, 'In protecting Islam in the manner we are, we are protecting all religions' (U.R. Rao, 1994, p. 296). At the same time, Gandhi was fully aware that in religious matters 'however sympathetic you may be, you cannot come to a correct decision on a matter of vital and religious importance to the parties concerned' (Robert Payne, 1969, p. 440). This is especially so in a conflict situation.

Gandhi himself traces the reason for this attachment with the religion in which one is born when he compares this attachment with and involvement in one's religion with the love and care for one's own wife. He says,

> I can no more describe my feelings for Hinduism than for my own wife. She moves me as no other woman in the world can. Not that she has no faults; I daresay, she has many more than I see myself. But the feeling of an indissoluble bond is there. Even so I feel for and about Hinduism with all its faults and limitations.
>
> (Ronald Duncan, 1983, p. 181)

This indissoluble bond between oneself and his religion is the cause of deep love for one's religion. As the Christian hymn declares:

> Love so amazing, so divine,
> Demands my soul, my life, my all.

This excessive, maddening, and possessive love is the cause for one's taking pride in and considering one's religion as superior to other religions and an exclusive repository of absolute truth.

Just as Gandhi swears by his religion and is ready to die for it, so are those who belong to other religions. Just as Gandhi over and over again justifies his actions by saying, 'My religion teaches me' (D. G. Tendulkar, 1951, p. 196), so are those belonging to other religions justified in taking refuge for their actions under the dictates of their religion. Like Gandhi, they may also invoke religious sanctions for justification of their deeds – or even misdeeds. As long as the followers of different religions are confined like a Robison Crusoe or like a frog in the well to their own religion and the practices dictated by it and remain within their personal, private, and individual lives, there may be no conflict. Nevertheless, the moment one enters the social arena, in public space one is bound to compare and contrast it with other religions, for the dictates of a religion are to be carried out by a group or a society that has entered into its folds, voluntarily or otherwise.

One of the most glaring religious conflicts that Gandhi faced in his life – and which to a large extent was the cause of division of India into two nations and the consequent human misery – was his interaction with Jinnah. Whereas Gandhi's view of religion was at least in part purely metaphysical or idealistic as discussed earlier, Jinnah's was purely empirical, realistic, rustic, and down to earth. In response to a letter from Gandhi in which he rejects a separate nation for the Muslims, Gandhi very chauvinistically says:

> I find no parallel in history for a body of converts and their descendants claiming to be a nation apart from the parent stock. If India was one nation before the advent of Islam, it must remain one in spite of the change of faith of a very large body of their children.
>
> (Yogesh Chadha, 1997, p. 403)

Jinnah argues:

> We maintain that Muslims and Hindus (have) distinctive culture and civilisation, language and literature, art and architecture, names and nomenclature, sense of values and proportion, legal laws and moral codes, customs and calendar, history and traditions, aptitudes and ambitions: in short, we have our own distinctive outlook on life.
>
> (Yogesh Chadha, 1997, p. 403)

Jinnah had maintained the same position in his address to the Muslim League session held in Lahore in March 1940 in which it was resolved to form a separate Muslim state by partitioning India. First, he denied that Hinduism and Islam are full-fledged religions in the Western sense and said:

> It is extremely difficult to appreciate why our Hindu friends fail to understand the real nature of Islam and of Hinduism. They are not religions in the strict sense of the word, but they are, in fact, different and distinct social orders and it is a dream that the Hindus and the Muslims can ever evolve a common nationality.
>
> (Yogesh Chadha, 1997, p. 368)

But later in the same speech admitting that the two are not only different and distinct religions but are diametrically opposed to one another, he continued:

> The Hindus and the Muslims have two different religious philosophies, social customs and literatures. They neither intermarry, nor interdine together, and indeed, they belong to two different civilisations which are based mainly on conflicting ideas and conceptions. Their aspects on life, and of life, are different. It is quite clear that the Hindus and the

34   *Ashok Vohra*

Muslims derive inspiration from different sources of history. They have different episodes. Very often, the hero of one is a foe of the other and likewise their victories and defeats overlap.

(Gandhi, *The Collected Works*, Vol. 78, *p. 178*)

Opposing Jinnah's interpretation of the opposition between Hinduism and Islam Gandhi said,

My whole soul rebels against the idea that Hinduism and Islam represent two antagonistic cultures and doctrines. To assent to such a doctrine is for me denial of God, for I believe with my whole soul that the God of the *Koran* is also the God of the *Bhagavad Gita*.

(Gandhi, *The Collected Works*, Vol. 21, p. 49; Gandhi, *The Collected Works*, Vol. 78, p. 132)

He asked Jinnah,

is Islam such an exclusive religion as Quaid-i-Azam would have it? Is there nothing in common between Islam and Hinduism or any other religion? Or is Islam merely an enemy of Hinduism? Were the Ali Brothers and their associates wrong when they hugged Hindus as blood brothers and saw so much in common between the two? I am not now thinking of individual Hindus who may have disillusioned the Muslim friends.

(Gandhi, *The Collected Works*, Vol. 78, p. 178)

Jinnah stubbornly refused to answer any of these queries.

When Jinnah a staunch advocate of division of India, the establishment of Pakistan said that the two nation theory was an 'article of faith' for him and his followers and 'we depend upon nobody except ourselves for the achievement of our goal'. For us the establishment of Pakistan is 'war to the knife'; Gandhi could do nothing except say, 'If Pakistan as defined (by Jinnah) is an article of faith with him, indivisible India is equally an article of faith with me. Hence there is a stalemate' (Gandhi, *The Collected Works*, Vol. 83, p. 124). About the expression 'war to the knife' he could say nothing but

'War to the knife' is a simple English idiom. I have never known it used in the literal sense. It simply means a determined quarrel between parties. I hold that if there is nothing in common between the two or nothing which does not come in conflict with each other's culture there can be no friendly mutual agreement.

(Gandhi, *The Collected Works*, Vol. 83, p. 427)

He pleaded to the Muslims in general and Jinnah in particular, 'Please do not regard me as an enemy of Islam and the Muslims here. I have always been a friend and servant of yours and of the whole world. Do not dismiss

Religious conflicts 35

me' (Gandhi, *The Collected Works*, Vol. 84, p. 199). Gandhi assured Jinnah and his followers that he had never 'had any design on Mussalmans' and 'betrayed their interests' and even put his life in the hands of Muslims when he said, 'My life is entirely at their disposal. They are free to put an end to it, whenever they wish to do so' (Gandhi, *The Collected Works*, Vol. 83, p. 191). When all pleadings failed to change Jinnah's mind he finally had to stop negotiations with Jinnah by saying, 'If Muslim raj is inevitable, then let it be; but how can we give it the stamp of our assent? How can we agree to the domination of one community over the others?' (Gandhi, *The Collected Works*, Vol. 83, p. 195). His idealistic views about religion, viz., 'Religion (binding faith), is made of sterner stuff; it is a deep personal matter, more personal than honour. To be true, it must be able to defy coercion of the extremists' type' (Gandhi, *The Collected Works*, Vol. 96, p. 134), could not hold ground in the face of such a stiff and committed opposition of Jinnah.

Gandhi did everything within his powers to resolve the conflict by persuasion – one of the most important components of his method of *satyagraha*. Even the other components of *satyagraha*, namely negotiations, self-purification, and direct action that Gandhi used for bringing about reconciliation between the two religious communities, as we all know, failed to bring about the desired results. However, as is well known, he failed miserably in making the opponent see his side of the argument, let alone actually winning him over. This was because one was talking at the empirical, ground reality level, while the other was talking at the metaphysical, philosophical level. This failure in bringing about reconciliation between Jinnah's conception and his own conception of the two religions made Gandhi admit his and his method's failure on this front. In another context in his statement to announce his twenty-one day fast from September 18, 1924, he acknowledged his failure in bringing about a harmony between the followers of the two religions and expressed his anguish by saying, 'Nothing evidently that I say or write can bring the two communities together' (*The Collected Works*, Vol. 25, pp. 171–172).

In his desperation for reconciliation and in the interest of Hindu-Muslim unity, Gandhi even said,

> I claim to be amongst the oldest lovers of Hindu-Muslim unity and I remain one even today. I have been asking myself why every wholehearted attempt made by all including myself to reach unity has failed, and failed so completely that I have entirely fallen from grace and am described by some Muslim papers as the greatest enemy of Islam in India. It is a phenomenon I can only account for by the fact that the third power, even without deliberately wishing it, will not allow real unity to take place. Therefore, I have come to the reluctant conclusion that the two communities will come together almost immediately after the British power comes to a final end in India.
>
> (Gandhi, *The Collected Works*, Vol. 84, p. 212)

36   *Ashok Vohra*

But alas, that was not to be. Gandhi was dismayed and completely shattered by the Hindu-Muslim riots that started soon after the attempts at reconciliation failed. Gandhi described the killing of Muslims by Hindus and that of Hindus by Muslims as 'madness tragic and shameful'. His appeal to both the communities that one of them should 'give up' fell on deaf ears. He could realise that he was wrong in presupposing that 'the innate goodness of human nature which perceives the truth and prevails during a crisis as if by instinct' (Gandhi, *The Collected Works*, Vol. 83, p. 204). At this juncture, following the advice given by Krishna to Arjuna in the *Bhagvadgita* 18.63, '*yathecchsi tathā kuru* – do as you like', Gandhi too left the matter to the individual to decide. He said, 'I want to live to see the day when this communal madness is forgotten. Whatever be our religion we should be Indians in action' (Gandhi, *The Collected Works*, Vol. 96, p. 79).

M. N. Roy, assessing the work and achievements of Gandhi after the latter's martyrdom, opines, 'like the other religious prophets of morality, peace and human brotherhood, Gandhi was destined to fail in his mission of bringing about harmony among the followers of different religions'. According to him, Gandhi's attempts at bringing about a harmonious relationship between religions were doomed and his method of *satyagraha* and *ahimsa* that succeeded and were effective in conflict resolution in the political and other arenas were headed for a failure on at least two counts. First, because being primarily a religious man he 'set before his followers high ideals which could not possibly be attained unless the human spirit broke out of the charmed circle of the religious mode of thought'. Second, because 'Communal harmony is not possible in the mediaeval atmosphere of religious orthodoxy and fanaticism' (Yogesh Chadha, 1997, p. 31). Jyoti Basu, the doyen of Marxists in India, met Mahatma Gandhi in August 1947 at the Hydari Manzil in Beliaghata in Calcutta. Basu asked Gandhiji about the course of action that CPI could take for quelling the riots. Gandhi advised, 'You should take out joint processions of Hindus and Mussalmans'. About sixty years later Jyoti Basu admitted, 'we gave Gandhiji's suggestion a try but it did not work. The joint processions . . . were broken up by dogmatists' (Gopal Krishna Gandhi, 2011, p. 134).

The intervention by the diehard dogmatists, radical fanatics, is possibly why to date religions of the world have failed to fulfil the hope reposed in them. Charles Bonney in his concluding lecture in the first Parliament of Religions held in Chicago more than a hundred years ago had expressed his expectations from different religions in the following words: 'Henceforth the religions of the world will make war, not on each other, but on the giant evils that afflict the mankind'. However, the religions have continued to wage a war against one another to establish their own superiority. Gandhi admitted in his autobiography, 'I had realised early enough in South Africa that there was no genuine friendship between the Hindus and the Mussalmans' (Gandhi, *The Collected Works*, p. 4). Nevertheless, he always made all efforts 'to remove obstacles in the way of unity' and always wished to act as 'the best

Religious conflicts   37

cement between the two communities'. It seems that Gandhi too realised that absolute unity between the two communities was impossible and supported the movements that made efforts 'not for uniting the religions, but for uniting hearts, despite the differences of religion' (Gandhi, _The Collected Works_, Vol. 19, p. 289). Gandhi rejected superficial attempts like intermarriage and inter-dining between Hindus and Muslims as methods of uniting the followers of two religions. First, because he upheld 'it to be utterly impossible for the Hindu and Mohammedans to intermarry and yet retain intact each other's religion' (Gandhi, _The Collected Works_, 19, p. 28). Second, because it was his 'settled conviction that . . . the causes of discord (between the two communities) are economic and political' (Gandhi, _The Collected Works_, 19, p. 31). It is clear from his following categorical assertion that all his efforts at bringing about a harmony among religions were at an individual level. He says,

> I claim to be _Sanātani_ Hindu. And I want to live at peace with my neighbours. I can only do so by serving them. I have no desire to save my country or my religion by killing others. I know that God will hold me blameless if He finds me capable of dying for either.
> (Gandhi, _The Collected Works_, 19, p. 382)

'Action is my domain, and what I understand, according to my lights, to be my duty, and what comes my way, I do. All my action is actuated by the spirit of service' (Gandhi, _The Collected Works_, Vol. 90, p. 1) substantiate it; the communal harmony comes into the domain of the individual efforts. This amounts to a confession of failure by a man who V. S. Narvane thought 'was fully aware of the nature of his power'.

Conclusion

Though Gandhian methods – _satyagraha_, _sarvodaya_, _swaraj_, non-violence – of conflict resolutions are very effective in the political matters, the same, however, are not able to resolve the religious conflicts. It is primarily because the foundation of a religious conflict is non-trust in the other, and the feeling of the minorities that the majority community will eventually smother them. The majority community feels that the minorities are clandestinely making inroads into their religions by adopting the technique of conversion. The common feeling that their respective religions are superior to the other and offer better explanation of the puzzles of life and efficient means of liberation, thus creating a mindset of exclusiveness, is the root cause of the conflict between them. These feelings can only be allayed by promoting the study of comparative religions, better communication, sincere dialogue among religions, and inculcating respect for universal human rights. The other reason for the failure of Gandhian methods in resolving the religious conflicts is that Gandhi did not realise that religious differences are not merely based on

38 Ashok Vohra

doctrinal metaphysical issues but are the outcome of perceived injustice, poverty, and unemployment of one religious community in relation to the other.

The Gandhian methods in this scenario fail to overcome the deeply ingrained mindsets founded on religion-based inimical relationships and fears, to unite hearts and infuse the spirit of common community fellow being, and the realisation of the fact that religion-based conflict can be self-defeating. In the matter of religious conflicts, once the mutual trust between the conflicting religions is lost for whatever reason, it is almost impossible to rebuild it and continue the negotiation, because the violent acrimonious minds with distrust leave little room for wisdom to understand.

Notes

1 The chapter is based on a VIRAJ Lecture delivered on February 12, 2016 at India Habitat Centre New Delhi.
2 According to him it is religion that teaches us that 'we should remain passive about worldly pursuits and active about godly pursuits, that we should not set a limit to our worldly ambition and that our religious ambition should be illimitable. Our activity should be directed into the latter channel' (*Hind Swaraj*, p. 37).
3 Faith, according to Sir Mohammad Iqbal, is 'the essence of religion' (Mohammad Iqbal, p. 1) .
4 When those belonging to other religions approached Gandhi to allow them to convert to Hinduism, he invariably told them not to do so and asked them to be a better Muslim, Christian, or Jew.
5 Alberuni noted, 'I used great care in examining every single one of them, in repeating the same questions at different times in a different order and context. But lo! what different answers did I get! God is all-wise' (Alberuni's India, p. 129).
6 Gandhi argued that the cruelties that are committed in the name of religion 'are not part of religion'. He put the blame of these religious wars and the consequent cruelties and massacres on the 'ignorant and credulous people' (Gandhi, 1909, p. 37).
7 Mohammad Iqbal extends this characteristic to all religions. He says, 'Religion can hardly afford to ignore the search for a reconciliation of the oppositions of experience and a justification of the environment in which humanity finds itself' (Iqbal, p. 2).

References

Alberuni, 1910, *Alberuni's India*, edited and translated by Edward C. Sachau, Kegan Paul, London.

Chadha, Yogesh, 1997, *Rediscovering Gandhi*, Century, London.

Desai, Valaji Govindji (Ed. and Trans.), 1960, *The Diary of Mahadev Desai*, Navajivan, Ahmedabad.

Duncan, Ronald (Ed.), 1983, *The Writings of Gandhi*, Fontana/Collins, UK, p. 181.

Gandhi, Gopalkrishna, 2011, *Of a Certain Age: Twenty Life-Sketches*, Penguin, New Delhi.

Gandhi, Mahatma M. K., 1909, *Hind Swaraj or Indian Home Rule*, Navajivan Publishing House, Ahmedabad.

Gandhi, Mahatma M. K., 1958, *The Collected Works of Mahatma Gandhi: Volume 1 to 100*, Publication Division, New Delhi.

Iqbal, Mohammad, 1975 (Reprint), *The Reconstruction of Religious Thought in Islam*, Oriental Publishers and Distributors, New Delhi.

Kriplani, Krishna, 1960, *All Man Are Brothers*, Navajivan, Ahmedabad.

Natesan, G.A., 1933, *Speeches and Writings of Mahatma Gandhi*, GA Natesan and Co., Madras.

Payne, Robert, 1969, *Life and Death of Gandhi*, E.P. Dutton, New York, p. 440.

Parel, Anthony J. (Ed.), 2009, *Gandhi: "Hind Swaraj" and Other Writings Centenary Edition*, Cambridge University Press, Cambridge.

Prabhu, R.K. and Rao, U.R. (Eds.), 1967, *The Mind of Mahatma Gandhi*, Navajivan Publishing House, Ahmedabad.

Rao, U.R. (Ed.), 1994, *The Way to Communal Harmony*, Navajivan Publishing House, Ahmedabad.

Tendulkar, D.G. 1951, *Mahatma*, Volume 2, edited by Vithalbhai Jhaveri and D.G. Tendulkar, Popular Prakashan, Bombay.

4 Interfacing Ambedkar and Gandhi[1]

Valerian Rodrigues

In contemporary Dalit-lore Ambedkar is generally pitted against Gandhi. Gandhi is seen as the votary of Hinduism and upper castes. He is also seen as the defender of the varna system, which in turn is interpreted as the matrix of the caste system. Over the years Dalit scholarship has adduced much documented evidence to demonstrate Gandhi's sustained resistance to consider Dalits as a distinct constituency in India's national life and accord them the appropriate representational weightage to overcome their social marginality (Vundru 2018: 41–57; 114–116). There is no dearth of narratives that project Gandhi as a wily opponent who trapped Ambedkar to sign the Poona Pact (1932) through his fast unto death by which Dalits became beholden to caste Hindus for political representation for good. One of the recent works that celebrates this antagonism is Arundhati Roy's introduction to Ambedkar's *The Annihilation of Caste* (A. Roy 2013: 15–180). While Roy tends to project Gandhi as the villain of the piece and Ambedkar as hero, there are others who while depicting Gandhi as the authentic other of colonial modernity have either seen Ambedkar as an apologist of colonialism or as an imposter (Shourie 1997).[2] There is a body of scholarship today that sees Ambedkar as a later-day votary of a thick modernist project in a postcolonial setting (Nagaraj 2010: 78),[3] while Gandhi himself is projected as someone contending against the epistemic and political project of modernity and striving to propose an alternative.[4] Against it I wish to argue that Gandhi and Ambedkar shared many concerns and ideas in common,[5] particularly the way they read the Indian society. However, their background assumptions and theoretical stances vastly differed, and consequently their policy prescriptions differed on a range of issues. This chapter subjects their intellectual and political legacies to a scrutiny and suggests a way of engaging with them.

Shared perspectives and concerns

Ambedkar and Gandhi shared much in common with regard to their understanding of human beings in general. They believed, although for different reasons, that human beings are endowed with a unique dignity and the capacity to define and reorient their lives. They also thought that social and

Interfacing Ambedkar and Gandhi 41

political institutions and processes can either enhance such endowments or mar their prospects. Therefore, enablement of people in general is integrally bound with revamping of social institutions. Both of them sought an affirmation of human agency rather than merely seeing it as subservience to forces beyond their control. Their ideas of opposition to human servility, non-domination, *swaraj* and gender equality were shaped by this shared conception. They prioritised an ethical stance to human action on this ground.[6]

It is not merely a set of ethical concerns that they shared in common but core philosophical orientations as well. A philosophical non-positivism was their common anchor: Human understanding and judgments are irreducible to the world of perception and the measurable. They accorded a priority to consciousness over our immediate sense-perception. The values and understanding that we carry overboard direct and shape our perception very intimately. Our ways of acting on the world and the priorities that we assign to an action over another are shaped by our understanding and our disposition to the world we are situated in. At the same time, acting on the world, sharing our experiences and deliberating and negotiating across them in our social world shape our understanding and reorient us to the world afresh. Such an approach makes both Gandhi and Ambedkar reject philosophical atomism[7] of an *Upanishadic* or a Cartesian kind and emphasises that human understanding is social and interactive. It would therefore be very unfair to box Ambedkar into the 'modernist' camp[8] and pit him against Gandhi.[9]

Both Gandhi and Ambedkar thought that their primary interest lies in shaping 'right' understanding and disposition to the world. According to them religion had tended to monopolise this domain, and under conditions of modernity, 'a scientific approach' is proposed in its place. They subjected both these domains, religion and science, to critique and called for revamping them. Their contention against the religious ideologies of their time or what went in the name of religion is well-known (Gandhi 1955; Ambedkar 2011). They also felt the need to distinguish between 'scientific approach' and 'scientific knowledge'. While they defended a scientific approach to reality, they felt that mere emphasis on scientific rationality and 'scientific' knowledge can reinforce domination and prove hugely detrimental to fostering the human.[10] At the same time both of them recognised the great significance of religion in social life. They asserted that religion is not personal but social, and our life will be bereft of the human if religion is shorn off it. Naturally such an understanding of religion does not see it as a creedal and ritual formation but a set of dispositions and orientations to our world, both natural and social. It would be very unfair to them to collapse their understanding of religion to any one of those currently vying for our souls and our final loyalties. There is little evidence to suggest that Ambedkar associated religion only with a Semitic version of the same.

Given their approach to human understanding, both Gandhi and Ambedkar laid much stress on education but considered the existing models of education inappropriate to nurture 'right' disposition and orientation.

42 Valerian Rodrigues

Ambedkar's call to 'educate, agitate and organise' placed education on priority[11] and Gandhi, apart from his wider and more encompassing perspective on education, proposed his idea of '*Nai Talim*' to cultivate a citizenship tuned to gainful earning while learning (Iyer 1987: 77–89, Vol. III).[12] However, given their differences with regard to the ends that human beings seek, they differed on the substantive understanding of education: Ambedkar identified human telos as *self-perfection*, which according to him was feasible only through social cooperation and recognition accorded in the process, while Gandhi saw such a telos in *self-knowledge* and *self-realisation* that demanded minimising our material wants and needs while according equal respect and concern to others.

The approach of Gandhi and Ambedkar to history reflects greatly their approach to human understanding. Ambedkar was primarily interested in identifying those factors that have become a road-block in the present for cultivating right understanding and dispositions. The approach to history and tradition therefore was from the present to the past rather than historicist, i.e., fathoming the laws of history. What we wish to be, rather than what we have been, was the question foremost before him.[13] He, therefore, employed his concerns of reason, morality and value-norms to read the past, endorse currents and modes of life and drub his adversaries. Within this framework, however, he insisted on meticulous gathering of data and evidence. He also employed this frame to characterize certain readings of history as interest-prone or prejudiced (Rodrigues 2011: 56–66) and others as the right way of doing so. For instance, he felt that the idea of equality is the 'sovereign virtue' of our times, and, employing it as the norm, tried to scan history and texts to find out to what extent they endorsed it or tried to subvert it. *Manusmriti* became his central text of ridicule since it classified human beings into superiors and subordinates and proposed an authoritative regimen to protect and reproduce such an order. It is interesting to point out that Gandhi's approach to history was akin to that of Ambedkar, i.e., access it from concerns significant to us in the present. However, he differed from Ambedkar on the issue of relative significances of concerns that made his substantive understanding of historical episodes markedly different. While Gandhi saw the *Bhagvad Gita* as the very embodiment of *satya* and *ahimsa* (Gandhi 1983: 14), Ambedkar saw it as a counterrevolutionary text that upheld the virtue of detachment to elicit subservience of the lower orders, still seeped in Buddhist lore, to a brahminical social dispensation (Ambedkar, 1987: 357–380).

Given their approach to history, both of them reveled in interpreting texts and traditions. They rejected positivist readings of texts and argued that it is important to take into account space, time and culture to understand them. They thought that all texts stand in need of interpretation and debated the methodology appropriate for the same. Gandhi also distinguished between a religious text that calls for certain disposition internal to a tradition and other texts. He also applied the same method to understand a religious tradition.

A sociologist studying a religious tradition would understand it differently from a believer who belongs to and identifies himself with such a tradition. Gandhi felt that alongside reason 'the eye of faith' is equally important to understand religious texts. Ambedkar, however, felt that that 'the eye of faith' could sustain partisanship and could be deeply prejudiced. He did not wholly reject an emotive attachment to texts and traditions (Ambedkar 2011: 63) but thought that it could only be grounded on the priority of reason. However, more than abstract principles of interpretation, Ambedkar and Gandhi focused on the reading of Hinduism and Buddhism. While the former felt that on the whole Hindu texts were concerned with defense of priest-craft, ritualism and social institutions that upheld graded social inequality, Gandhi thought that these texts and traditions have nurtured great spiritual heritage and led people to pursue the path of truth rather than untruth. Gandhi also felt that they contained self-corrective resources within themselves. Ambedkar, however, was little convinced of Gandhi's argument and pointed out the great social evils, such as untouchability, that Hinduism harboured within itself. He also saw Buddhism as diametrically opposed to mainstream Hinduism, while Gandhi argued that the Buddha is integral to the Hindu tradition.[14]

Political stances

Unlike most other nationalist leaders, Gandhi was deeply aware of the limited social base of the national movement in India. One of his early initiatives was to expand the base of the national movement by reaching out to the peasantry and the industrial working class (Brown 1974). But Gandhi also recognized the need to eradicate the social practice of untouchability; build Hindu-Muslim alliance; and shore up the means of livelihood of people and instill a sense of pride in them by employing their skills and time by reviving Khadi, cottage and village industries. Such inclusive nationalism received fulsome praise from Ambedkar. Ambedkar and Gandhi, however, differed with each other with regard to the methods to be employed for such inclusion.

Gandhi argued that untouchability is an evil that the upper castes have inflicted on the untouchables, and the former have to make reparation for the same. Those who perform an immoral act must make amends for it. He found no sanction for untouchability in the Hindu scriptures. Untouchability is a practice that has crept into Hinduism as its corruption. Gandhi adduced little evidence to prove that untouchability is not integral to Hinduism, but he built up the argument, as was his wont, that Hinduism, given the spiritual and moral heights that it conquered, could not have engendered an evil of the kind that untouchability was. Predictably, Ambedkar and many others perceived such a stance of Gandhi as an attempt to protect Hinduism rather than develop self-help among untouchables themselves. He also argued that one's own humanity cannot be left to the mercy of others who have a vested interest in denying it. On the Hindu-Muslim

44 Valerian Rodrigues

tension, Gandhi thought that many religions could co-habit the same political space, mutually learning from each other. One cannot claim one's own religion as superior to that of others but live his religion as bequeathed to him or her. While Ambedkar agreed with Gandhi that religious belonging does not necessarily beget national bond, he thought that it is important to take preemptive measures against such a development, if many religious communities wish to live in a common fold. With regard to the means of production and distribution of produce, while Gandhi recognized that there were social classes within the fold of the Indian nation, he felt that eventually the owners of the means of production could be persuaded to voluntarily act as the trustees of the people under their charge. Ambedkar exemplified self-help among untouchables and sought to enhance the sphere and significance of ordinary life in which all participate irrespective of their religious belonging. He argued that the existing mode of social production is invariably based on social classes with class struggle as its inevitable outcome. He also argued that concentration of resources in a few hands can affect rights and liberties of people deleteriously. He sought resolution of the class-conflict by taking recourse to a mode of radical democracy which, among other concerns, determines the contours of the economy rather than it being left to the fancy of the market.

Politically, Gandhi and Ambedkar were much in agreement with regard to three issues: the significance of non-violence, the role of masses and the idea of *swaraj*. Ambedkar decried use of force and coercion as political means since they are not appropriate for human bonding and could do more harm than good, be short-sighted and reinforce authoritarianism. Unlike Gandhi, who considered non-violence as an end in itself, Ambedkar argued that it was a means to ends independently stipulated. Whether means or end, the arguments that they advanced in justification of non-violence have much in common. Ambedkar's critique of Indian nationalism was on grounds of its being exclusive, and he thought that it should be made inclusive by uprooting social institutions founded on gradations and ranking and by enabling people to decide their own futures. *Swaraj* is a term that occurs in Ambedkar far too often, largely as a critique of the narrow idea of nationalism upheld by the Congress. He saw *swaraj* as a public virtue and not a personal state of being, and it cannot be promoted by keeping those it encompasses outside the fold:

> In the fight for swaraj you fight with the whole nation on your side. In this (annihilation of caste) you have to fight against the whole nation and that too, your own (nation). But it is more important than swaraj. There is no use having swaraj, if you cannot defend it. . . . In my opinion only when the Hindu Society becomes a casteless society that it can hope to have strength enough to defend itself. Without such internal strength, Swaraj for Hindus may turn out to be only a step toward slavery.
>
> (Ambedkar 2010: 80)

The economy

Much of the existing commentary on Ambedkar's approach to the economy presents his ideas as far removed from that of Gandhi. There is some truth in such a representation since Ambedkar had major differences with Gandhi with regard to economic policies and even approach to the economy as a whole. All these differences apart, both of them did not want the human to be reduced to instrumental rationality in the name of modernity and technology. Gandhi argued that man has a telos above and beyond the earthly paradise that discourse on development has dished out. He therefore sought an economy that could be under the collective control of its users, and he felt that it should have its base at the lowest level of a political and administrative unit (Mantena 2012a: 540). In other words, Gandhi's politics sought to be at the driver's seat as far as his economics was concerned. *Swaraj* was a state where a person or a collective was in control of its own resources, its needs, its skills and competences. Gandhi therefore believed that a decentralized economy made of rural produce and village, cottage and Khadi industries would be much more conducive to *swaraj*. He also thought that by giving a moral turn to enterprise through the ideal of trusteeship, age-old social capital and entrepreneurship would remain intact while curbing the instinct of profit and aggrandizement of resources, for its own sake. Much of the application of his politics to the economy cannot be sustained, but there is a sterling thought in his approach to the economy, that the machine is made for man and not man for the machine: The kind of economy that a society chooses should be its choice rather than the economy dictating its terms to it.

While Ambedkar is often celebrated as an economist, and he did some excellent research on public finance and currency,[15] he saw economic initiatives and public policy as political choices rather than the other way about.[16] His approach to the agrarian question, big industry, planning, labour policy, resettlement and ecological questions were largely premised on his politics outlined earlier. Unlike Gandhi, Ambedkar was not opposed to large scale production or to modern technology but wanted to wet them with the distinct concerns and politics that he avowed.[17]

Approach to Indian society

The closest that Gandhi and Ambedkar came to each other is in the categories they employed and the concerns they upheld regarding Indian society and the language they deployed for popular communication. Unlike subsequent iconisation, many things they said and did were not acceptable to their audiences, but they understood each other very well. The issues and concerns that Ambedkar raised were remarkably akin to those of Gandhi: Nature of *swaraj*, social inequality, moral basis of power, human enablement, relation between religion and politics, sensitivity to diversity and inclusion, gender equality, the direct role of masses in politics and an openness to the world.

46 *Valerian Rodrigues*

In fact, the frame that they employed to understand India and diagnose its ailments employed such conceptual categories as caste, untouchability, gender, rural-urban, religion, social institutions, Hindu-Muslim question, human dignity and equality, *swaraj* and *satyagraha*, education, learning and deliberation, and dissent and protest. While they recognised the force of nationalism they hedged it in through other qualifiers. They saw politics as an inclusive activity of social transformation and discovery of self. There were very few who thought on similar categories. The systems of thought that they proposed in the process were far removed from their liberal and Marxist counterparts and laid down the foundations for the non-West to speak on its own terms.

Political action

Both Gandhi and Ambedkar believed that political action can be profoundly transformative. They invested much in engendering a collective human agency that is politically viable and effective and bestowed much attention in forging politically viable organisations. In fact, Gandhi called politics the religion of our times. The transformative nature of political action is not merely confined to overhauling social relations but also values, beliefs, and dispositions and the inner self too. Both of them called for mass action for the purpose and did meticulous planning to ensure that it achieves the desired goals. While they differed with regard to the understanding of *satyagraha*, both of them took recourse to it when the existing channels of redressing grievances proved inadequate. Both of them were ever ready to call into question emerging modes of dominance, even though they might have arisen as the consequences of their very action.

Contention and conflict

We need to take into cognizance the basic disagreements between Ambedkar and Gandhi while tracing the ground that they shared in common. While they have much in common with regard to the idea of the human, they differed greatly with regard to its substantive content. Look at the way Ambedkar positions his perspective on the issue: Human beings, to be as such, need to be socially recognised. Only in and through such recognition does he or she come to realise his or her strengths and weaknesses. Human perfection becomes possible only by being related to wider and denser levels of human interaction, which he termed, using John Dewey's term, 'social endosmosis'. The caste system, particularly untouchability, by treating people not merely as inferior but also as defiling, confines and limits such interactions. The kind of labour they are associated with, their habitations, the denial of the sacral, social prohibitions and prescriptions and the ascription of pollution to their presence instill among untouchables a negative sociality. There is no light for them at the end of the tunnel, except the promise of a better next life, if they

Interfacing Ambedkar and Gandhi   47

submit themselves to the injunctions of the social order.[18] Ambedkar would have extended this argument to say that all social structures and relations that come in the way of the expansive reach of a person are hurdles in his or her way of striving towards their perfection.

Gandhi did not think that it is essential to develop wider and thicker levels of social cooperation and interaction for human perfection. In fact, wider levels of social cooperation would enhance a person's material needs and requirements that would prove to be an affront to self-rule. Limiting one's needs and regulating social division of labour for the purpose was essential to subservient *swaraj*.[19] For Gandhi the process of discovery of one's own self also attunes one to the rest of the world. Behind their respective approaches to social cooperation there were foundational differences between Gandhi and Ambedkar with regard to the concept of the human person. For Gandhi the human person was given, while for Ambedkar humans became human through social interaction, realising their potentialities in the process.

Ambedkar and Gandhi found themselves at a crossroads while evaluating the modern turn. Ambedkar saw in it immense prospects for striving after human perfection. Modern reason can instill confidence in human beings and undermine supernaturalism and ritualistic practices. Modern industry and professions can be conducive to human enablement, if they are appropriately employed. Gandhi thought otherwise: The modern turn invariably throws up roles, structures and instrumentalities that bind men and women in new chains. Under it human needs and wants inevitably tend to be expansive, reinforcing structures of violence all round. For Gandhi colonialism was one of its expressions. However, the end of colonial rule will not bring *swaraj*, although it is an essential precondition for the latter. The ideal of *swaraj* would continue to be the norm even under national independence.

For Ambedkar democracy becomes the large theatre where human potentialities are unfolded. To the contrary, for Gandhi the reconstitution of social life should involve as little dependence as possible on wider social networks. He argued that striving to *reconstitute* social life should accord priority to spiritual pursuits. For Gandhi the varna system was not an affront to human equality but an ideal that mandated pursuit of callings that one is embedded in, without their being superior or inferior (Mehta 2011). Untouchability is definitely an offence, while the labour that an untouchable performs is a social need. What is important, therefore, is to inform all kinds of labour with dignity. The *Bhangi* will continue to be *Bhangi*, but the valuation that we ascribe to her labour should undergo a change. Unlike Gandhi, Ambedkar thought that caste Hindus do not regard untouchability as a distortion or aberration but as integral to their religious beliefs and practices. Caste system and the *varna* system avow the same principle. Both of them are founded on the principle of graded inequality, which find their sanction in key texts of the tradition that Hindus regard as sacrosanct. These systems have not let lower castes and particularly untouchables access wider horizons. Contra Gandhi, he felt that caste Hindus were unlikely to commune with the untouchables.

48 *Valerian Rodrigues*

Given this social disposition, should the untouchables wait for the change of heart of the upper castes to claim their humanity? Gandhi countered such a stance, saying that rights are claims that are upheld by the conscience of a society. Without a change in the perspective of the upper castes, a unilateral pursuit of their claims by the untouchables will precipitate massive violence from the former (Rodrigues 2011: 62).

Their differing understanding of the human, social institutions, democracy and modernity led Ambedkar and Gandhi to assign very different significances to state power. Ambedkar stressed the autonomy of the state and its accountability to democracy. Constitutional democracy became the mode of negotiating this relation. He was deeply apprehensive of the state falling victim to social prejudice and dominance. Only an autonomous state will be able to ensure rule of law mandated by a democratic dispensation. Gandhi saw an autonomous state as an instrument of violence and dominance pitted against *swaraj*, as self-determination. For him the reason of the state can only be promotion of *swaraj* (Mantena 2012a: 552–553).

Given the difference in their understanding of the role of public power, Gandhi and Ambedkar found themselves poles apart on issues such as *Panchayat Raj* or local autonomy of power. Ambedkar sought equality, freedoms and democracy at the local level, as elsewhere in social relations, although he thought that certain prerequisites such as cultural compactness and linguistic bond were essential for the purpose. He saw the existing Indian village as caught in domination, inequity, violence and narrowness of outlook, characteristics that bode ill for human striving in general and that of the marginalised in particular. Countering the demand that the village be made as the primary unit of India's constitutional edifice, he retorted, 'What is the village but a sink of localism, a den of ignorance, narrow-mindedness and communalism' (*Constituent Assembly Debates* 2004, Vol. 11:6 Vol. VII, p. 39). He argued that only a constitutional democracy can be the enabling condition for civilised striving at the local level. Gandhi, however, saw the village as a site of social cooperation that ideally should provide everything that a man or a woman needs for everyday life. He saw it as essential for *swaraj*. Writing in *Harijan* of 26 July 1942, he outlined his conception of the village as follows:

> My idea of village swaraj is that it is a complete republic, independent of its neighbours for its vital wants, and yet inter-dependent for many others in which dependence is a necessity. Thus, every village's first concern will be to grow its own food crops and cotton for its cloth. It should have a reserve for its cattle, recreation and playground for adults and children. . . . The village will maintain a village theatre, school and public hall. It will have its own waterworks. . . . As far as possible every activity will be conducted on a cooperative basis. There will be no caste, such as we have with· their graded untouchability. Non-violence with its technique of satyagraha and non-cooperation will be the sanction of the

village community. . . . The government of the village will be conducted by the Panchayat of five persons annually elected by the adult villagers, male and female, possessing minimum prescribed qualifications. These will have all the authority and jurisdiction required. Since there will be no punishments in the accepted sense, this Panchayat will be the legislature, judiciary, and executive combined to operate for its year in office. Any village can become such a republic without much interference.

(Iyer 1987: 263–264, Vol. III)

Given this understanding, Gandhi sought 'ever-widening, never-ascending circles', 'not a pyramid' but 'an oceanic circle' of social interaction with the 'individual as its centre' (Iyer 1987: 232, Vol. III). While Gandhi was talking of his ideal village and Ambedkar of the actual, the tension between them on this issue was real and revolved around their foundational differences with regard to human striving, nature of *swaraj* and idea of democracy.

The contention between Ambedkar and Gandhi was drawn from and fed into their differences with regard to culture and tradition. Ambedkar saw the teachings of the Buddha as the benchmark to read culture and traditions and Brahmanism as an ideology pitted against it. He thought that any retrieval of India's past can only be on the basis of the benchmark of Buddha's teachings. Gandhi differed: He argued that search for truth through the path of non-violence was central to the Hindu tradition, and Buddha's teachings were integral to such a search. Everything else was subject to interrogation.

Conclusion

We have argued earlier that there was much in common between Ambedkar and Gandhi not merely on substantive issues but also the epistemic framework they employed. The categories and concepts that they deployed to understand Indian society had much in common and definitely much more than any of their other counterparts. Both of them, in their own distinct ways, did not regard the colonial and modernist categories as adequate or even appropriate to understand the social reality of India or that of mankind as a whole. Both of them affirmed the creative potentiality of human agency to transform the world and called upon it not to succumb to the reason of the structures. At the same time we cannot ignore the profound differences between them on such issues as the idea of the human and the significance of the modern. While Ambedkar ardently championed the idea of an expansive democracy, Gandhi upheld the ideal of *swaraj*. They differed in their understanding of state, rule of law and constitutionalism. Above all they differed on assigning culpability and responsibility for social degeneration and evil in India. While Ambedkar singled out Brahmanism as the principal adversary and saw Buddhism as the moral terrain of advance, Gandhi thought that Hinduism is capable of reforming itself from within and saw Buddhism as integral to Hinduism.

50   *Valerian Rodrigues*

Notes

1 The essay is based on a VIRAJ lecture delivered on February 12, 2015 at India Habitat Centre New Delhi.
2 Such charges against Ambedkar had already become commonplace in the nationalist discourse and are reflected in such works as C. Rajagopalachari (1946) and K. Santhanam (1946).
3 In spite of some brilliant insights on Ambedkar and the Dalit movement, D. R. Nagaraj places Ambedkar centrally in the modernist camp, while presenting Gandhi as addressing the distinct cultural sensitivity of India. He says that while 'Gandhi represents the traditional Indian mode of tackling the problem of untouchability', Ambedkar represents 'the modern Western mode and is closer to militant socialist methods of the Western variety' (Nagaraj 2010: 78). He sets up the axis of 'Ambedkar-Marxist tradition' for the purpose (Ibid, 202). Similarly, Kancha Ilaiah in many of his writings has alluded to Ambedkar as a strong votary of modernity (see Iliah 2009, 2010).
4 One thing that is constant in these critical studies is their attempt to distance Gandhi from what they regard as mainstream modes of thought in the trans-Atlantic world. The works of Faisal Devji (2012), Akeel Bilgrami (2003), Ajay Skaria (2017), Karuna Mantena (2012a, 2012b) and Uday Singh Mehta (2010, 2011) are significant in this regard.
5 One of the recent works that engages with the reciprocity and contestation between Ambedkar and Gandhi, an engagement that the author believes rewrites the relations across the foundational concepts of the 'political', is Aishwary Kumar's *Radical Equality: Ambedkar, Gandhi* and *the Risk of Democracy* (2015). Relative to this study, the scope of this chapter is limited and focuses on a set of specific concerns. The author, however, has disagreements with Kumar with regard to 1) the intellectuals antecedents of Ambedkar, 2) the interpretation of key concepts of the political domain and their relations in the writings of Ambedkar and Gandhi and 3) the zones of agreements and disagreements between the two. Given the nature and scope of these disagreements, this chapter can hardly be expected to interweave this critique. Incidentally, this chapter was initially drafted before Kumar's work was available to the author.
6 While numerous writings of Gandhi can be cited to corroborate such a stance, the key texts in this regard are: *Gandhi's Autobiography or The Story of My Experiments with Truth* (1927) and Mahadev Desai, edited, *The Gospel of Selfless Action, or The Gita according to Gandhi* (1946). For Ambedkar such texts are 'What it is to be an Untouchable' (1989), 'Buddha and Future of His Religion' (2003a) and the heart-touching essay by V. Geetha, 'Bereft of Being: The Humiliations of Untouchability' (2009).
7 The term 'philosophical atomism' is employed here to denote disengaged reasoning removed from the cultural matrix.
8 Representative comments are as follows: 'Ambedkar was an unalloyed modernist. He believed in science, history, rationality and above all, in the modern state for the actualization of human reason' (Chatterjee 2006: 77).
9 D. R. Nagaraj charts such a trajectory (Nagaraj 2010: 21–60). Nagaraj working on Kannada Dalit literature argues that much of this literature is caught in a binary split between Dalits pitted against Hinduism, and this split is largely drawn from the Ambedkarite-Marxist ideological legacy. In opposition to an holistic understanding of Hinduism inclusive of Dalits, to which Gandhi too contributed, Ambedkar defined 'Dalits as the products of an exclusivist and adversarial Buddhist past' (Ibid, 201). There were radical scientists inspired by Marxism who reveled in this opposition. However, their attempt to assume such an exclusivist position too has not succeeded since they could not explain 'the dominating

Interfacing Ambedkar and Gandhi 51

presence of anti-Dalit structures in the culture of the untouchables' (Ibid, 202). The exclusivist understanding contributed to the triumph of conservative forces since it led to 'denying the cultural and spiritual presence of untouchables and other lower castes on the site of Indian culture' (Ibid, 202). Dalit sensitivity to such perceived exclusion reacted with 'rage and fury' on one hand and 'self-pity and self-denial' on the other, and this was reflected in Dalit literature.

In this context Nagaraj bemoans the fact that

> Indian Renaissance was built on negating and silencing dissident, parallel, and alternative discourses developed by the lower castes and outcaste Brahmins who had revolted against orthodoxy. The tension that existed between the utter contempt towards untouchables as a social group on the one hand, and the uneasy encounter with their metaphysical and mystical worlds at the levels of non-orthodoxical religious practices on the other, was resolved in favour of the socially arrogant upper castes. The mystical worlds of Allama Prabhu, Sarhapa, Kanhapa, and Hadipa were withdrawn from the task of representing the lower castes.
>
> (Ibid, 202)

10 The debate between Gandhi and Ambedkar, following the publication of the latter's book, *The Annihilation of Caste*, makes this issue very clear. For the debate, see Ambedkar (2010: 81–96).

11 For Ambedkar education implied much more than what is generally implied by the term: It was the principal means of assigning dignity to oneself, inventing and defining oneself and developing resources to overhaul social relations: 'For ours is a battle, not for wealth or for power. It is a battle for freedom. It is a battle for the reclamation of human personality. . . . My final words of advice to you is educate, agitate and organize, have faith in yourselves and never lose hope' (Ambedkar 2003b: 276).

12 On Gandhi's wider approach to education see Raghavan Iyer, *The Moral and Political Writings of Mahatma Gandhi*, Vol. III, Oxford, Clarendon, 1987, pp. 377–389. He gave a definitive form to his idea of 'earning while learning' in his experiments of 1937.

13 According to Ambedkar, 'the Hindus must consider whether they should conserve the whole of their social heritage or select what is helpful and transmit to future generations only that much and no more. Prof. John Dewey, who was my teacher and to whom I owe so much, has said: "Every society gets encumbered with what is trivial, with dead wood from the past, and with what is positively perverse. . . . As a society becomes more enlightened, it realizes that it is responsible *not* to conserve and transmit the whole of its existing achievements, but only such as make for a better future society"' (Ambedkar 2010: 79).

14 In his speech at the Young Men's Buddhist Association at Colombo in 1927, he argued, 'Gautama was himself a Hindu of Hindus. He was saturated with the best that was in Hinduism, and he gave life to some of the teachings that were buried in the Vedas . . . Buddha never rejected Hinduism, but he broadened its base. He gave it a new life and a new interpretation' (Iyer 1986: 493, Vol. 1).

15 Ambedkar's two doctoral dissertations, *The Evolution of Provincial Finance* London, King and Co., 1925 and *The Problem of the Rupee* London, King and Co., 1923 at Columbia University and London School of Economics, respectively, focussed on these themes.

16 One of the concise statements in this regard are two of Ambedkar's writings, 'Mr Russell and the Reconstruction of Society' (Ambedkar 2010: 481–492) and 'States and Minorities' (Ambedkar 2010: 381–452).

52   *Valerian Rodrigues*

17 Some of the recent works that discuss Ambedkar's economic thought are Jadhav (1991: 980–82), Jadhav (1992) and Jadhav (2015); his approach to public policy is discussed in Abraham (2002: 4772–4774), Arya and Choure (2014: 84–86), Thorat (1998), Thorat and Aryama (2007) and Thorat and Kumar (2009); and his perspective on social discrimination has inspired Thorat (2002: 572–578), Thorat (2009), Thorat and Attewell (2007: 4141–4145), Thorat and Dubey (2012: 43–53), Thorat and Newman (2010) and Deshpande (2011) etc.
18 Ambedkar develops this argument in several texts, particularly in 'The Annihilation of Caste' (Ambedkar 2010: 23–98) and *The Buddha and His Dhamma* (Ambedkar 2011).
19 Gandhi outlines such a conception of self in several of his writings (see, for instance, CW 22:108; CW 32:150 etc.). For some useful comments on this issue see Parel (2006: 12–13), Mantena (2012a), Mehta (2011) etc.

References

Abraham, P. 2002. 'Notes on Ambedkar's Water Resources Policies', *Economic and Political Weekly*, 37(48): 4772–4774.
Ambedkar, B.R. 1987. 'Krishna and His Gita', *BAWS*, 3: 357–380.
Ambedkar, B.R. 1989. 'What It Is to Be an Untouchable', *BAWS*, 5: 3–34.
Ambedkar, B.R. 2003a. 'Buddha and Future of His Religion', *BAWS*, 17(2): 97–108.
Ambedkar, B.R. 2003b. 'Educate, Agitate, Organize, Have Faith and Lose No Hope', *BAWS*, 17(3): 273–276.
Ambedkar, B.R. 2010. 'The Annihilation of Caste', in *Babasaheb Ambedkar Writings and Speeches (BAWS)* (Vol. 1, 2nd ed.). Mumbai: Government of Maharashtra: 23–98.
Ambedkar, B.R. 2011. *The Buddha and His Dhamma: A Critical Edition*, edited by Aakash Singh Rathore and Ajay Verma. New Delhi: Oxford University Press.
Arya, Rajendra Kumar, and TapanChoure. 2014. 'The Economic Thoughts of Dr. Bhimrao Ambedkar with Respect to Agriculture Sector', *Developing Country Studies*, 4(25): 84–86.
Bilgrami, Akeel. 2003. 'Gandhi, the Philosopher', *Economics and Political Weekly*, 38(39): 4159–4165.
Brown, Judith. 1974. *Gandhi's Rise to Power: Indian Politics 1915 to 1922*. Cambridge: Cambridge University Press.
Chatterjee, Partha. 2006. 'B.R. Ambedkar and Troubled Times of Citizenship', in V. R. Mehta and Thomas Pantham (eds.), *Political Ideas in Modern India*. New Delhi: Sage: 73–90.
Constituent Assembly Debates, 2004. Vol. 11. New Delhi: Lok Sabha Secretariat.
Desai, Mahadev. 1946. *The Gospel of Selfless Action, or the Gita According to Gandhi*. Ahmedabad: Navajivan.
Deshpande, Ashwini. 2011. *The Grammar of Caste*. New Delhi: Oxford University Press.
Devji, Faisal. 2012. *The Impossible Indian: Gandhi and the Temptation of Violence*. Cambridge MA: Harvard University Press.
Gandhi, Mahatma K. 1927. *Autobiography or the Story of My Experiments with Truth*. Ahmedabad: Navajivan.
Gandhi, Mahatma K. 1955. *My Religion*. edited by B. Kumarappa. Ahmedabad: Navajivan.

Gandhi, Mahatma K. 1983. *Discourses on the Gita*, translated by Valji Govindji Desai. Ahmedabad: Navajivan.

Geetha, V. 2009. 'Bereft of Being: The Humiliations of Untouchability', in Gopal Guru (ed.), *Humiliation: Claims and Context*. New Delhi: Oxford University Press: 95–107.

Ilaiah, Kancha K. 2009. *Post-Hindu India: A Discourse in Dalit Bahujan Socio-Spiritual and Scientific Revolution*. New Delhi: Sage.

Ilaiah, Kancha K. 2010. *The Weapon of the Other: Dalitbahujan Writings and the Remaking of Indian Nationalist Thought*. Delhi: Longman.

Iyer, Raghavan. 1986. *The Moral and Political Writings of Mahatma Gandhi*, Vols. 1. Oxford: Clarendon.

Iyer, Raghavan. 1987. *The Moral and Political Writings of Mahatma Gandhi*, Vol. 3. Oxford: Clarendon.

Jadhav, Narendra. 1991. 'Neglected Economic Thought of Babasaheb Ambedkar', *Economic and Political Weekly*, 26(15): 980–982.

Jadhav, Narendra. 1992. *Dr Ambedkar: Economic Thoughts and Philosophy*. Mumbai: Popular Prakashan.

Jadhav, Narendra. 2015. *Ambedkar: An Economist Extraordinaire*. New Delhi: Konark.

Kumar, Aishwary. 2015. *Radical Equality: Ambedkar, Gandhi and the Risk of Democracy*. Stanford: Stanford University Press.

Mantena, Karuna. 2012a. 'On Gandhi's Critique of the State: Sources, Contexts, Conjunctures', *Modern Intellectual History*, 9(3): 535–563.

Mantena, Karuna. 2012b. 'Another Realism: The Politics of Gandhian Nonviolence', *American Political Science Review*, 106(2): 455–470.

Mehta, Uday Singh. 2010. 'Gandhi on Democracy, Politics and the Ethics of Everyday Life', *Modern Intellectual History*, 7(2): 355–371.

Mehta, Uday Singh. 2011. 'Patience, Inwardness, and Self-Knowledge in Gandhi's *Hind Swaraj*', *Public Culture*, 23(2): 417–429.

Nagaraj, D.R. 2010. *The Flaming Feet and Other Essays: The Dalit Movement in India*. Ranikhet: Permanent Black.

Parel, Anthony. 2006. *Gandhi's Philosophy and the Quest for Harmony*. Cambridge: Cambridge University Press.

Rajagopalachari, C. 1946. *Ambedkar Refuted*. Bombay: Hind Kitabs.

Rodrigues, Valerian. 2011. 'Reading Texts and Traditions: The Ambedkar-Gandhi Debate', *Economic and Political Weekly*, 44(2): 56–66.

Roy, Arundhati. 2013. 'The Doctor and the Saint', An Introduction to B.R. Ambedkar, *Annihilation of Caste*. New Delhi: Navayana: 15–180.

Santhanam, K. 1946. *Ambedkar's Attack, a Critical Examination of Dr. Ambedkar's Book: "What Congress and Gandhi Have Done to the Untouchables"*. New Delhi: Hindustan Times.

Shourie, Arun. 1997. *Worshipping False Gods: Ambedkar and the Facts Which Have Been Erased*. New Delhi: ASA.

Skaria, Ajay. 2017. *Unconditional Equality: Gandhi's Religion of Resistance*. London: University of Minnesota Press.

Thorat, Sukhdeo. 1998. *Ambedkar's Role in Economic Planning and Water Policy*. New Delhi: Shipra.

Thorat, Sukhdeo. 2002. 'Oppression and Denial', *Economic and Political Weekly*, 37(6): 572–578.

54   Valerian Rodrigues

Thorat, Sukhdeo. 2009. *Dalits in India: Search for a Common Destiny*. New Delhi: Sage.

Thorat, Sukhdeo, and Aryama (eds.). 2007. *Ambedkar in Retrospect: Essays on Economics, Politics and Society*. New Delhi: Rawat.

Thorat, Sukhdeo, and Paul Attewell. 2007. 'The Legacy of Social Exclusion', *Economic and Political Weekly*, 42(41): 4141–4145.

Thorat, Sukhdeo, and Amaresh Dubey. 2012. 'Has Growth Been Socially Inclusive during 1993–94 to 2009–10', *Economic and Political Weekly*, 47(10): 43–53.

Thorat, Sukhdeo, and Narendra Kumar (eds.). 2009. *B. R. Ambedkar: Perspectives on Social Exclusion and Inclusive Policies*. New Delhi: Oxford University Press.

Thorat, Sukhdeo, and K. Newman (eds.). 2010. *Blocked by Caste: Economic Discrimination in Modern India*. New Delhi: Oxford University Press.

Vundru, Raja Sekhar. 2018. *Ambedkar, Gandhi and Patel: The Making of India's Electoral System*. New Delhi: Bloomsbury.

5 Gandhi's imaginations of Muslims[1]

Hilal Ahmed

Introduction

Gandhi's attitude towards Muslims (especially the Muslims of colonial India) is often analyzed in two very different ways. On the one hand, Gandhi's views on religion, particularly on Islam, are recognized as 'foundational principles' to comprehend his political position(s) on Muslims.[2] Gandhi's close relationship with his Muslim associates (such as Maulana Abdul Kalam Azad, the Ali brothers, Hakim Ajmal Khan and others), Gandhi's strident support for Khilafat movement in 1920s and his pro-minority position in post-partition India are put together to construct an image of a 'secular' Gandhi.[3] Arguments of this kind, somehow, ignore the significance of Gandhi's practice-centric, context-specific imagination of religious communities.

There is another dominant thesis, which revolves around Gandhi's political moves, especially in the 1940s. This thesis brings in the notion of 'Muslim appeasement' to argue that Gandhi's soft attitude towards Muslims offered legitimacy to the League's separatism. This was the reason, we are told, why Gandhi failed to stop the partition of the subcontinent.[4] This *instrumentalist* reading of Gandhi (and for that matter the Partition of India) is also reflected in the writings of Hindu nationalists, including M. S. Golwalkar.[5]

This chapter does not subscribe to these very different sets of arguments. It explores Gandhi's imagination of Muslims of India by examining his changing conceptions of modern religious communities in a colonial context. The chapter looks at the ways in which Gandhi interprets India's Muslims as an identifiable religious group and asks a simple question: Why did Gandhi virtually pay no attention to the empirically evident Muslim socio-religious plurality?

This question has a wider academic relevance. Scholars such as Mohammad Mujeeb, T. N. Madan, Imtiaz Ahmad, Gail Minault and later Asghar Ali Engineer and Mushirul Hasan have argued that Islamic homogeneity was nothing but a political project that communalized the Indian society, and as a result the country was divided in 1947.[6] The communalism, they suggest, could only be defeated if we recognize Muslim plurality and various versions of 'lived Islam', which would, eventually, pave the way for a truly secular India. The figure of Gandhi comes time and again in these writings – either

56   Hilal Ahmed

as a champion of Hindu-Muslim unity or as the *Father of Nation*, a complete Hindu, whose politics was defeated by a 'culturally Muslim' Jinnah, who was not at all interested in Islam.

This portrayal of Gandhi is complicated. Gandhi continued to use Hindu-Muslims as legitimate political categories throughout his political career. Even during the Partition riots, he spoke of Muslims as a homogeneous entity. In his prayer meeting of 12 September 1947, Gandhi said:

> Let us know our own dharma. In the light of our dharma I would tell the people that our greatest duty is to see that the Hindus do not act in frenzy, nor the Sikhs indulge in acts of madness. . . . I appeal to the Muslims that they should open-heartedly declare that they belong to India and are loyal to the Union. If they are true to God and wish to live in the Indian Union, they just cannot be enemies of the Hindus. And I want the Muslims here to tell the Muslims in Pakistan who have become the enemies of the Hindus, not to go mad: 'If you are going to indulge in such madness, we cannot co-operate with you. We will remain faithful to the Union, and salute the tricolour. We have to follow the order of the Government'.
>
> (*CWMG*, Vol. 89, 01 August 1947–10 November 1947, p. 176)

This statement clearly identifies Muslims as one group of people that could now be divided into two categories: the Muslims who stay back in India and the Muslims who have migrated to Pakistan.

Was Gandhi not a victim of the colonial knowledge systems that conceptualized Indian communities as homogeneous entities? Was he not doing a different type of community politics (if not communal!) by intermixing religion and politics? Why did he overlook Muslim plurality as legitimate empirical evidence to respond to the Muslim League's claim that Hindus and Muslims were two nations, and therefore there was no scope for composite nationalism? Did his emphasis (or overemphasis) on Hindu-Muslim question strengthen the discourse of communal politics?

These questions might not be important for Gandhi. But, the ways in which Muslims plurality is posed as a righteous, ultimate, secular, political project by postcolonial Indian scholarship on Islam and Muslims forces us to trace Gandhi's imagination of Muslims.

Two clarifications are important for clarifying scope of this chapter. First, the chapter does not intend to reproduce the well-known story of Gandhi and his Muslim comrades. On the contrary, my purpose is to build an argument in the backdrop of this well-documented history of *Congress/nationalist Muslims*. Thus, the ideas, actions and political positions of Azad, the Ali brothers and Khan Abdul Ghaffar Khan are not discussed here. Second, the chapter does not claim to construct a neat and clean theory of Islam/ Muslims. Instead, an attempt is made to extract relevant fragments from Gandhi's writings to offer an explanatory sequence to them. This exercise,

Gandhi's imaginations of Muslims   57

I believe, would help us to open up new theoretical opportunities with regard to the researchers on Muslims of postcolonial India.

How to read Gandhi?

We find one interesting quote by Gandhi in most of the books published by the Navajivan Trust on the writings of Gandhi.
  Gandhi says:

> I would like to say to the diligent reader of my writings . . . that I am not at all concerned with appearing to be consistent . . . therefore, when anybody finds any inconsistency between any two writings of mine, if he has still faith in my sanity, he would do well to choose the later of the two on the same subject.
>
> (*Hind Swaraj*, 1938, p. 2)

Gandhi's advice is crucial. He wants us to contextualize his writings in their own historical contexts for extracting those possible meanings that he would have preferred. At the same time, this contextualization should not be seen as a direct submission to any given 'chronology of life events'. Gandhi, it seems, is keen to introduce his readers to the slow and gradual unfolding of his context-specific arguments. He, thus, functions not merely as an author in the conventional sense of the term but also an active participant in the evolving discourses around his writings and speeches.[7]
  Prathama Banerjee, Aditya Nigam and Rakesh Pandey suggest a creative possibility to deal with thinkers like Gandhi. They argue that a thinker must be understood in his/her context but at the same time, 'by liberating a thought from its context . . . we can actually mobilize the possibilities that it might open up in contexts vastly different from its past conditions of emergence' (Banerjee et al., 2016, p. 49).
  Following this suggestion, I read Gandhi's writings and speeches on Muslims, at least in the chapter, in three different ways: I read Gandhi in relation to the events that provoked him to respond to certain larger questions; I read Gandhi in relation to the intellectual resources – the political concepts, administrative categories and religious-cultural discourses – that were available to him and finally, I read Gandhi in relation to the contemporary portrayal of Muslims as a homogeneous entity, which is posed as a natural enemy of democracy and peace.

Muslims as bullies

Let us begin with *Hind Swaraj* – the small pamphlet that Gandhi wrote in 1909 and the only complied version of his ideas that he did not wish to change or disown. There is an interesting conversation between the reader and the editor about the inborn enmity between Hindus and Muslims. Gandhi, the editor in this episode, argues with the reader that expression such

58   Hilal Ahmed

as 'inborn enmity' emerged only after the advent of British Raj. Describing Muslims as an inseparable constituent of Indian nation, Gandhi says:

> Should we not remember that many Hindus and Mahomedans own the same ancestors and the same blood runs through their veins? Do people become enemies because they change their religion? Is the God of the Mahomedan different from the God of the Hindu? Religions are different roads converging to the same point. What does it matter that we take different roads so long as we reach the same goal? Wherein is the cause for quarrelling?
>
> (*Hind Swaraj*, 1938, p. 46)

He further says:

> Those who do not wish to misunderstand things may read up the Koran, and they will find therein hundreds of passages acceptable to the Hindus; and the Bhagavadgita contains passages to which not a Mahomedan can take exception. Am I to dislike a Mahomedan because there are passages in the Koran I do not understand or like? . . . If everyone will try to understand the core of his own religion and adhere to it, and will not allow false teachers to dictate to him, there will be no room left for quarrelling.
>
> (*Hind Swaraj*, 1938, p. 48)

This portrayal of Muslims as a peace-loving Indian religious community and the Quran as a message of peace and love goes well with our postcolonial minority-rights driven sensitivities. Any post-Indira Gandhi Congress style self-declared secular leader might find this passage valuable to score a point over Hindutva *bhakts* of our times.

However, this was not the case with Gandhi. He was absolutely sure that one must have to make a crucial distinction between the religious discourses and everyday forms of lived religion. In 1924 when a series of communal riots broke out in northern and western India, a group of Muslims met Gandhi and proposed a workable solution to stop communal violence. They suggested that Hindus should recognize the Prophet Mohammad as a prophet and Allah as almighty God; and Muslims should pay equal respect to Lord Ram and Lord Krishna and appreciate the Vedas as a divine book. This mutual respect for religious texts and icons, they anticipated, would encourage communities to come together and shun violence. Gandhi very categorically rejected this proposal. He writes:

> The solution was not quite so simple . . . (it) . . . might be good enough for the cultured few, but it would prove ineffective for the man in the street. For the Hindus cow-protection and the playing of music even near the mosque was the substance of Hinduism, and for the Mussalmans cow-killing and prohibition of music was the substance of Islam.
>
> (*CWMG*, Vol. 25, August 1924–January 1925, p. 178)

Gandhi's imaginations of Muslims 59

In Gandhi's opinion, thus, the common Hindus and Muslims follow a religion that is far away from the moral teachings of Hinduism and Islam. Therefore, expecting that the reforms in religion would function instrumentally and transform the followers of that religion is an artificial premise.

One may argue that there is slight contradiction in Gandhi's views. In *Hind Swaraj*, he establishes a direct link between religious texts and followers of Islam. But, in 1924, he seems to be convinced that actual conducts in the name of religion are different from the moral teachings of religion. This is a valid contradiction even from the point of view of Gandhi himself. The ideas expressed in *Hind Swaraj* cannot be rejected by following the advice Gandhi offers about the sequential logic of his writings.

Akeel Bilgrami offers us an interesting theoretical solution to this kind of puzzles. Bilgrami argues that Gandhi's thought 'was highly integrated, his ideas about very specific political strategies in specific contexts flowed (and in his mind necessarily flowed) from ideas that were very remote from politics. They flowed from the most abstract epistemological and methodological commitments' (Bilgrami, 2003, p. 4159). If we agree with Bilgrami's observation, we have to then explore those 'epistemological' commitments that provide a certain kind of integrity of ideas with regard to Indian Muslims.

Gandhi wrote a long article entitled *Hindu-Muslim Tension: Its Causes and Cure* in *Young India* in May 1924. The tone of this article is unusually provocative. It talks of certain universally applicable characteristics of Hindus and Muslims and even goes on to justify the use of violence for the sake of self-defense.

Gandhi describes Muslims as *bullies* and Hindus as *cowards*. He says:

> There is no doubt in my mind that in the majority of quarrels the Hindus come out second best. My own experience but confirms the opinion that the Mussalman as a rule is a bully, and the Hindu as a rule is a coward. I have noticed this in railway trains, on public roads, and in the quarrels which I had the privilege of settling. Need the Hindu blame the Mussalman for his cowardice? Where there are cowards, there will always be bullies. . . . Whose fault was this? Mussalmans can offer no defence for the execrable conduct, it is true. But I as a Hindu am more ashamed of Hindu cowardice than I am angry at the Mussalman bullying. Why did not the owners of the houses looted die in the attempt to defend their possessions? . . . My non-violence does not admit of running away from danger and leaving dear ones unprotected. Between violence and cowardly flight, I can only prefer violence to cowardice.
>
> (CWMG, Vol. 24, May 1924–August 1924, pp. 141–142)

As expected, this provocative description of Hindus and Muslims was condemned widely.[8] The Hindu readers of his journal criticized him for being partial to Muslims while Muslim readers blamed him for preaching violence.

60   Hilal Ahmed

Gandhi, however, does not accept these criticisms. In the next issues of *Young India* he reproduced some of these letters with his rejoinder. He said:

> I fail to see anything dangerous in my writing. I should be glad indeed if my statement energizes the Hindus to defend themselves in the face of danger. We may not expect unity before we cease to fear one another. . . . I can understand the necessity of not washing every rag of dirty linen in the open, but we cannot afford to slur over things that stare us in the face and of which everybody thinks.
>
> (*CWMG*, Vol. 24, May 1924–August 1925, p. 235)

This series of conversation between Gandhi and his English-educated Muslim readers is full of insightful comments and the nature of communal violence. But, quite surprisingly the depiction of Muslims as a fighter community or 'bullies' does not turn out to be a point of contention in these exchanges. Was *bully* not a negative expression?

Muslims as a courageous *qaum*

This question leads to us the popular description of Indian religious communities. Most of the upper castes of Muslims, we must remember, were always kept in the official category called the 'martial races'. Interestingly, the cultural values and religious beliefs of these upper castes of Muslims eventually came to be recognized as the social characteristics of all Muslims in India. I take three examples to illustrate this point.

John Strachey's famous text *India* offers us an exciting description of Muslims of India. The book, which was published in 1891, talks of Muslim sociological heterogeneity with a remarkable clarity. Strachey finds that Muslims are not entirely Islamic. He says that the most of the Muslims 'are ignorant of the religion to which they nominally belong, and so little devoted to its tenets, that they might almost as properly be counted among the innumerable classes of Hindus' (Strachey, 1894, p. 235). He further clarifies this general observation: 'the dominant races of Pathans and Baluchis are of foreign origin, but majority of the population consists of the decedents of Hindus or aboriginal tribes, who long accepted, more or less, the religion of their conquerors' (Strachey, 1894, p. 235).

We have now two kinds of Muslims: the foreigners, the warriors and those who won India and the local Muslims who were converted to Islam long back but who are not fully Islamic. The foreigners, Strachey notes,

> hold a more influential position in the country than their mere numbers would give them; they are . . . energetic than Hindus, and possess greater independence of character. In perfection of manner and courtesy a Mohammedan gentleman of Northern India has often no superior.
>
> (Strachey, 1894, p. 240)

Gandhi's imaginations of Muslims   61

The distinction between India's Muslims and the ruling tribes of Muslims, Strachey argues, evaporates in the 19th century when the movements to 'purify Islamic faith' among Muslims begins. In his opinion, 'the more orthodox a Mohammedan becomes the wider becomes the gulf that separates him from every form of idolatrous worship' (Strachey, 1894, p. 241). It is, therefore, expected that purification of Islam would not merely produce a homogeneous Muslim community but also empower them to imbibe the courage and determination of ruling classes.

This observation was not entirely incorrect. Writing about the specificities of racial and religious characteristics of Muslims, leading Islamic scholar Ameer Ali underlined the fact that Muslims were the only homogeneous community in colonial India. In a long essay, *Racial Characteristics of Northern India and Bengal*, published in 1907, Ali argues that the 'bond of common religion and unity of tradition constitute the Muslims into perhaps the only homogeneous nationality in India' (Ali, 1968, p. 294). This spectacular oneness, he suggests, produces a remarkable pride. In Ali's opinion, Muslims' *'manliness is only partly racial. In a great measure it springs from his religion, which inspires him with a sense of human dignity and independence'* (Ali, 1968, p. 234, emphasis added).

Ameer Ali does not ignore the sociological and cultural plurality of Muslims of India. He classified Muslims of India into four caste like groups – Syed, Mughal, Pathan and Sheikh. He gives details of the first three groups, highlighting the history of their settlement in India, their cultural values and social formations. For instance, Syed are described as nobles, Pathan as mighty and courageous, and Mughal as custodians of high culture. However, he does not find it useful to talk about Sheikhs. He says: 'in the term Sheikh are included the descendants of the converts – from Hinduism and settlers from the west who do not belong to other groups. *No particular reference to their characteristics seems necessary'* (Ali, 1968, p. 246, emphasis added).

This intentional omission of Sheikhs, the local converts, is very significant. Ameer Ali, it seems, strongly believes that this group of Muslims is not entirely Islamic. In fact, they are in the processes of 'becoming Muslims'! Like Strachey, he also feels that Muslim culture and identity can only be defined in purely Islamic terms if the history of the Muslim nation (*qaum*) is rewritten and publicized and the lower strata of Muslims are introduced to superior racial values of upper caste Muslims – the Syed, Pathan and Mughal.

The centrality of Islamic history in defining what Iqbal calls the spirit of Muslim culture was not limited to high politics of colonial administration. A purified conception of Islam as a powerful intellectual resource influenced not merely the Islamic reform movements of 19th century but also the evolving literary traditions, especially the Urdu poetry. Iqbal's famous poem *Shikwa*, which was first recited in 1911 in the annual *jalsa* of the

62 *Hilal Ahmed*

Anjuman-Himaya-e-Islam, Lahore, seems to capture these intricacies of Islamic identity with a remarkable originality. In *Shikwa* (Complaint to God), he writes:

इसी मामूरे में आबाद थे यूनानी भी
इसी दुनिया में यहूदी भी थे नसरानी भी
पर तेरे नाम पे तलवार उठाई किसने
बात जो बिगड़ी हुई थी वो बनाई किसने

In that same region, the Greeks too dwelled.
In that same world, the Jews too, the Christians too
But who lifted a sword for Your name?
The affair that had gone awry – who fixed it up?

(Iqbal, 2006)

Two years later in 1913, he wrote *Jawab-e-Shikwa* (Response to a Complaint) that was first recited in a *Mushaira* at Mochi gate, Lahore. In this long poem he evokes the point of view of God. The God, in this poem, asks Muslims to become more Islamic:

वज़्अ में तुम हो नसारा तोतमद्दुन में हुनूद
ये मुसलमाँ हैं जिन्हें देख के शरमाएँ यहूद
यूँ तो सय्यद भी हो मिर्ज़ा भी हो अफ़ग़ान भी हो
तुम सभी कुछ हो बताओ तो मुसलमान भी हो

If in manner you are Christian, then in culture, Hindu!
These are the Muslims! – On seeing whom, the Jews would be ashamed!
As it happens, you are Sayyids, you are Mirzas too, you are Afghans too –
You're everything – tell me, are you Muslims too?

(Iqbal, 2006)

If one looks closely at these examples, Strachey's text book for civil servants introducing them to the everyday world of Muslims in India, Ameer Ali's scholarly description of the racial character of Muslim nation and Iqbal's *Muslim* anxiety expressed in a poetic language, we might discover two very essential aspects of the process of Islamization that aimed at making Muslims of India more Islamic. The effort to discover as well as popularize a pure, unadulterated, universal Islam had been a prime objective of religious reformers and those who were keen to define Muslims as a nation. At the same time, there was a search for history to classify values, practices and rituals into Islamic and un-Islamic. Consequently, an imagination of an informed, ideal and pure Islam and an equally historicized portrayal of Muslim community emerged in the colonial public discourse of the early 20th century. An image of a highly religious, pious, strong, independent, war-loving Muslim Pathan, in fact, eventually became the dominant identity markers of Muslims of India in contrast to the docile, feminine and unorganized (though educated!) Hindus. The question here is: Did Gandhi subscribe to this abstract representations of Hindus and Muslims uncritically?

Muslims versus Islam

Let us go back to the debate that began in 1924 and continued for the next three years in the pages of *Young India* and *Navajivan*. In a long article Gandhi argues that the character of Muslims as a religious community should not be confused with Islamic morality that he discovers in the Quran. Nevertheless, he finds Muslims to be bullies because of two possible reasons.

First, there is a *mystified* story of Islam that establishes the fact that Islam cannot be envisaged without violence and the rule of sword. Gandhi finds this 'distorted' version of Islam highly problematic. He argues:

> The sword is no emblem of Islam. . . . Islam was born in an environment where the sword was and still remains the supreme law. The message of Jesus has proved ineffective because the environment was unready to receive it. So, with the message of the Prophet. The sword is yet too much in evidence among Mussalmans. It must be sheathed if Islam is to be what it means – peace. . . . Reliance upon the sword is wholly inconsistent with reliance upon God. There should be, on their part, unequivocal mass condemnation of the atrocity.
>
> (CWMG, Vol. 32, November 1927–January 1927, p. 475)

Second, the *history of imperialism* associated with Islamic expansion, Gandhi argues, transformed Muslims into an aggressive community.

> The Mussalman, being generally in a minority, has as a class developed into a bully. Moreover, being heir to fresh traditions, he exhibits the virility of a comparatively new system of life. Though, in my opinion, non-violence has a predominant place in the Koran, the thirteen hundred years of imperialistic expansion has made the Mussalmans fighters as a body. They are therefore aggressive. Bullying is the natural excrescence of an aggressive spirit.
>
> (CWMG, Vol. 24, May 1924–August 1924, p. 270)

Thus, Gandhi clearly poses a serious challenge to the process of growing Islamization among Muslims. He reminds us that the moral principles given in the Quran and the history of Muslims are different from each other. He seems to call upon Muslims to think of a different possibility: discovery of Islam without relying on the given Muslim history of violence and conquest.

To understand this contempt for history, we have to go back to the *Hind Swaraj*. Gandhi makes a crucial distinction between past and history.

64   *Hilal Ahmed*

He finds that the enterprise of modern history does not have a place for what he calls love-force or soul force.

> It is . . . necessary to know what history means. The Gujarati equivalent means: 'It so happened.' If that is the meaning of history, it is possible to give copious evidence. But, if it means the doings of kings and emperors, there can be no evidence of soul-force or passive resistance in such history. . . . History, then, is a record of an interruption of the course of nature. Soul-force, being natural, is not noted in history.
>
> (*Hind Swaraj*, 1938, pp. 73–74)

It does not mean that Gandhi ignores the significance of having an understanding of the past. Gandhi imagines a past, which offers us a possibility to feel it, to think through it and to imbibe it in our actions.[9] He reminds us that 'to believe that what has not occurred in history will not occur at all is to argue disbelief in the dignity of man. At any rate, it behaves us to try what appeals to our reason' (*Hind Swaraj*, 1938, 61).

Gandhi seems to apply this imagination of the past to demystify the figure of the Prophet and other Islamic icons. In an essay published in *Young India*, Gandhi very categorically argued that the life of the Prophet Mohammad exemplified a straggle for justice, peace and equality.

Gandhi notes:

> I became . . . convinced that it was . . . the rigid simplicity, the utter self-effacement of the Prophet, the scrupulous regard for pledges, his intense devotion to his friends and followers, his intrepidity, his fearlessness, his absolute trust in God and his own mission. These and not the sword carried everything before them and surmounted every obstacle.
>
> (*CWMG*, Vol. 25, August 1924–January 1925, p. 127)

Despite this reverence for the Prophet, Gandhi makes a serious attempt to dig out moral principles from the stories weaved around these great religious icons. Writing about Caliph Umar, he argues:

> I fear that the acts of this great and just man are being presented to the Mussalman masses in a most distorted fashion. I know that if he rose from his grave, he would disown the many acts of the so-called followers of Islam which are a crude caricature of those of the great Umar himself.
>
> (*CWMG*, Vol. 25, August 1924–January 1925, p. 127)

Gandhi's creative reading of the Quran and the life of Islamic figures, particularly of the Prophet, empowers him to think of an independent context-oriented and reason-based Islamic morality, which, he seems to expect, does not contradict with his imagination of Truth and Ahimsa.

Gandhi's imaginations of Muslims   65

Does it mean that Gandhi was eventually a *textualist*, who finds every solution of the problems of Muslims in the creative re-reading of the Quran?

Islam of a Hindu

Gandhi very confidently asserted his moral right as a Hindu religious person to talk about the Quran, the life of the Prophet Mohammad and at the same time the moral religious decline of Muslim communities. On a number of occasions Gandhi made it clear that Muslims were not the exclusive proprietors of the message of Islam.

This evocation of universally applicable Islamic ethnics is compatible with Gandhi's meanings of religion. Gandhi notes, 'all religions are more or less true. All proceed from the same God, but all are imperfect because they have come down to us through imperfect human instrumentality' (*CWMG*, Vol. 24, May 1924–August 1924, p. 149).

Islam, in this sense, is also an imperfect religion. However, in order to understand the moral teachings of Islam, Gandhi seems to suggest, one must de-historicize the Quran and demystify the figure of the Prophet Mohammad and first four Caliphs. Responding to an incident in which two Ahmediyaa Muslims were stoned to death in Afghanistan, Gandhi openly criticized this practice. He writes:

> I understand that the stoning method is enjoined in the Koran only in certain circumstances which do not cover the cases under observation. But as a human being living in the fear of God I should question the morality of the method under any circumstance whatsoever. Whatever may have been necessary or permissible during the Prophet's lifetime . . . *this particular form of penalty cannot be defended on the mere ground of its mention in the Koran. Every formula of every religion has in this age of reason, to submit to the acid test of reason and universal justice if it is to ask for universal assent. Error can claim no exemption even if it can be supported by the scriptures of the world.*
>
> (*CWMG*, Vol. 26, January 1925–April 1925,
> p. vii, emphasis added)

Here, Gandhi takes a radical position. Elaborating the distinction between religion and believers of religion, he brings in the question of reason and universal justice. The teachings of the Quran, therefore, are to be examined in relation to the moral-cultural values of society.

Gandhi's experiments in Noakhali were the ultimate test of this conviction. In the riot-affected areas of Noakheli, where a large number of people (especially Hindus) were killed in October 1946, Gandhi decided to stay in Muslim dominated villages. Here he did some highly unusual experiments of *Bhramcharya* (celibacy), especially with his 18-year-old granddaughter, Manu. He started sharing a bed with Manu without wearing any piece of cloth.

66   *Hilal Ahmed*

The commentaries on these *Bhramcharya* tests do not pay adequate attention to the *Muslim* context in which Gandhi performed these conscious experiments.[10] In fact, a section of Gandhi's followers and close associates (including those who eventually were called *Gandhians* in the later period, such as Vinoba Bhave) repudiated Gandhi's action. They found it morally outrageous and politically undesirable (Lal, 2000, pp. 115–117). All references to Gandhi's ideas and actions with regard to sexuality, hence, become those 'detrimental issues', which should not be talked about at all.

It is important to remember that violence against women – rape, abduction, molestation and forced conversion – emerged as a new form of communal politics in the 1940s. For someone like Gandhi, who had been experimenting with his body for a long time and whose body had already acquired a public presence of its own, sexual violence posed a new set of challenges. From his point of view, condemnation of an act of violence is nothing but a moral criticism, which is different from moral judgement – a position that one takes after internalizing the nuances of the act itself.[11]

Gandhi's diary note of 2 January 1947 clarifies this distinction between moral criticism and moral judgement. He writes: 'I can see there is some grave defect in me somewhere which is the cause of all this. All around me is utter darkness. When will God take me out of this darkness into His light?' (*CWMG*, Vol. 86, 21 October 1946–20 February 1947, p. 302). Here Gandhi relates his bodily self with the acts of violence around him. This *internalization* is further employed to produce a bodily act so as to arrive at a moral judgement on the act of violence, in this case, sexual violence.

Gandhi's two intrinsically linked moves in Noakheli – his peace work among Muslims and his *Bhramcharya* experiments with Manu – therefore cannot be compartmentalized. This goes against the *integrity* of Gandhi's proposal – the search for an intrinsic unity of thought and action. Noakheli was a Muslim dominated belt of East Bengal. Gandhi had gone there as a practicing Hindu to advise Muslims to give up violence. And in the middle of this peace mission, he was deeply involved in what he calls 'an ultimate yajna' – eventually a bodily act.

The description of a public meeting in Amishparathat published in *Harijan* is very significant. The meeting was held on 1 February 1947. A Muslim Maulavi wanted to speak before Gandhi simply to counter Gandhi's views on Islam and Muslims. Gandhi allowed him to make a short speech before him. Maulavi argued that Gandhi's views on *Purda* were anti-Islamic, and as a Hindu he did not have any right to make any comment on Muslims and Islam. Maulavi also said that the slogan *Rama-Rahim* was objectionable: Rahim referred to Allah while Rama was simply a name of a king.

Gandhi responded to these objections in firm manner. He refused to accept this 'narrow view' of Islam and argued that 'Islam was not a creed to be preserved in a box. It was open to mankind to examine it and accept or reject its tenets'. Gandhi further claimed that Rama and Krishna were not the names of ordinary human beings as 'Man worshipped the same God under different

Gandhi's imaginations of Muslims 67

names and the Koran was not opposed to it' (*CWMG*, Vol. 86, 21 October 1946–20 February 1947, pp. 420–421).

In the concluding part of this speech, Gandhi talks of his *Bharmcharya* experiments. It is reported:

> Gandhiji referred to 'small-talks, whispers and innuendos' going round of which he had become aware. He was already in the midst of so much suspicion and distrust, he told the gathering, that he did not want his most innocent acts to be misunderstood and misrepresented. He had his granddaughter with him. She shared the same bed with him. The Prophet had discounted eunuchs who became such by an operation. But he welcomed eunuchs made such through prayer by God. His was that aspiration. It was in the spirit of God's eunuch that he had approached what he considered was his duty. It was an integral part of the *yajna* he was performing and he invited them to bless the effort. He knew that his action had excited criticism even among his friends. But a duty could not be shirked even for the sake of the most intimate friends.
>
> <div align="right">(<i>CWMG</i>, Vol. 86, 21 October 1946–20
February 1947, pp. 420–421)</div>

We do not know how this passage of his speech, which was delivered in Hindustani, was translated in Bengali and how Muslims who gathered there responded to it. But the invocation of the figure of the Prophet Mohammad by underlining the most unheroic Islamic category, the Muslim eunuchs, in a way, a highly innovative intellectual exercise.

The modern Islamic religious discourses in India do not openly talk of those pious companions of the Prophet, whose gender was uncertain. It simply goes against the heroic description of Islamic expansion and the *manliness* of Muslim *umma*. However, Gandhi continued to use the figure of 'Muslim eunuch' as a legitimate expression to substantiate his understanding of a true Muslim. In his written speech at Atakhora on 19 January 1947, Gandhi quoted Prophet Mohammad for describing a pious Muslim as *eunuch*.[12] He writes:

> Muslims are those who perform their trust and fail not in their word and keep their pledge. . . . He is not a Momin who commiteth adultery or stealeth, or who drinketh liquor or who plundereth or who embezzleth; beware, beware. The most excellent jehad is that for the conquest of self. Assist any person oppressed, whether Muslim or non-Muslim. The manner in which my followers become *eunuchs* is by fasting and abstinence.
>
> <div align="right">(<i>CWMG</i>, Vol. 86, 21 October 1946–20 February 1947, p. 372)</div>

Was Gandhi juxtaposing Muslim *bullies* with a humane, docile, submissive and outcaste figure of a pious eunuch?

68 Hilal Ahmed

Conclusion

Let us reassemble the conceptual fragments that we extract from Gandhi's writings on Muslims to respond to the main thrust of this chapter: Gandhi's use of Muslims as a homogeneous entity.

Gandhi, as I have pointed out, recognizes the unfolding of two modern processes: the identification of Muslims communities precisely on the basis of religion for governmental purposes and Islamization of Muslims to make them inseparable part of a pan-Islamic community. These two processes actually set out the terms of social, political and cultural discourses. In such a scenario, Gandhi does not spoil his energies in denouncing the modes in which Muslims were presented; instead, he chooses to rework on the concept of Muslim itself. However, unlike liberal modernists of his age, Gandhi does not go in the realm of history to find out the exact, true and fixed meanings of Islam and an ideal and prescribed religious behavior for Muslims.

On the contrary, he explores multiple meanings of religious texts such as the Quran. This highly elucidated rereading allows him to *de-historicize* Islam and *demystify* the figure of the Prophet. The de-historicized Islam enables Gandhi to discover the moral meanings of religious texts, which constitute the everyday forms of Islamic religiosities in different contexts. Hence, without overtly emphasizing plurality of Muslim communities, Gandhi introduces us to a highly diversified imaginations of the Quran itself, which is considered as a revealed book, the word of Allah, which can never be changed or amended. His emphasis on the purification of individual self opens up immense possibilities to even go beyond the revealed *truth* of the Quran.[13]

Similarly, the demystified image of the Prophet Mohammad made it possible for Gandhi to highlight the emptiness of given Muslim homogeneity. Unlike Jinnah, who could not produce a sustainable argument for Muslim unity in 1940s despite his equally powerful rejection of the past, Gandhi was able to discover a humane face of lived Islam.[14] The reference to Prophet's *eunuch* in Gandhi's framework destabilizes the Muslim Leagues' parity argument that 'mighty Muslims of India (simply in terms of numbers) constitute a modern nation and therefore they need a state of their own'. Gandhi, it seems, poses a radically different question: What is the status of the most marginalized sections of Muslims in League's conception of Muslim unity? This question is posed in more direct fashion by underlining the equally powerful distinction between discursively constituted Islamic morality (who is a pious Muslim!) and actual conducts of Muslims. In other words, Gandhi reminds us that there is a possibility of thinking multiple forms of valid and legitimate Islamic *homogeneities* without compromising with the universally celebrated principles of Islam.[15] This creative imagination of Muslims of India, I argue, makes Gandhi our contemporary.

Notes

1 I am thankful to Dr. S K Srivastava, Dr. Y. P. Anand and my colleagues at CSDS for their encouragement, critical comments and suggestions for this chapter.

2 In an essay on Gandhi and Islam, Amit Dey argues: 'theology, if studied in its proper historical setting with a multidisciplinary approach, can yield results. Though such an approach is still in its infancy in India, if used it can provide a more comprehensive picture of a historical event or historical personality' (Dey 2013, p. 31).

3 I do not wish to overemphasize Gandhi's role in the Khilafat movement as a reference point to understand his imagination of Muslims/Islam. However, at the same time, I would like to argue that his active role in the Khilafat movement introduced him to the complexities of Islamic identity more directly. He became aware of the crucial distinction between an imagined Islamic oneness and the actual sociological, cultural and national diversity of Muslims. In order to contextualize his political support for the Turkish control over the holiest religious places of Islam, Gandhi proposed a very creative argument. He writes, 'if I understand the spirit of Islam properly, it is essentially republican in the truest sense of the term. Therefore if . . . Arabia desired independence of Turkey they should have it . . . complete Arabian independence would mean transference of the khilafat to an Arab chieftain. Arabia in that sense is a Mussulman trust, not purely Arabian. And the Arabs without ceasing to be Mussulman, could not hold Arabia against Muslim opinion. The khalifa must be the custodian of the holy places and therefore also the routes to them. He must be able to defend them against the whole world. And if an Arab chief arose who could better satisfy that test than the Sultan of Turkey, I have no doubt that he would be recognized as the khalifa' (*CWMG*, Vol. 18, p. 72). Here, Gandhi tries to *demystify* the status of Khalifa by invoking the 'republican' spirit of Islam. I shall elaborate this idea of 'demystifying the symbols of Islam' in the later part of the chapter.

4 Y. G. Bhave's book, *Mahatma and the Muslims* (1997), is a relevant example of this kind of writings.

5 In his book the *Bunch of Thought*, Golwalkar says, 'The more our leaders tried to appease the Muslims, the more their separatist and aggressive appetite was whetted. The British too set about to sharpen their separatist teeth and claws in a bid to set them against the nationalist forces. Thus Muslims were placed in a position in which they were wanted by both the British and the nationalist and their price was rising higher and higher' (Golwalkar, 1966, p. 122).

6 See Mujeeb (1967), Madan (2011), Ahmad (1983), Minault (1982), Hasan (1997) and Engineer (1975).

7 For a detailed discussion on *How to Read Gandhi*, especially with regard to *Hind Swaraj*, the texts he wrote in 1909 and did not change or edit its subsequent editions, see Parel (2007).

8 For an elaborated analysis of Hindu cowardice as a concept, see Rudolph and Rudolph (2010, pp. 160–183).

9 Sunil Khilnan's essay *Gandhi and History* is very relevant to explore Gandhi's imagination the past.

10 Vinay Lal's brilliant essay on Gandhi's imagination of sexuality tries to offer a contextual reading of Gandhi's experiments. Lal (2000, pp. 107–108).

11 For an elaborated discussion on this point, see Bilgrami (2003).

12 One may argue, in my view quite legitimately, that the figure of Muslim eunuch must also be read in relation to Gandhi's conceptions of gender. The discussion on 'Muslim women', thus, opens up another conceptual space. I accept this possible limitation of this chapter. I also find that Gandhi evokes 'Muslim women' with regard to the *Parda* debate on a number of occasions. Yet, *Muslim women* are not

70   *Hilal Ahmed*

fully conceptualized as a radically distinctive category in Gandhian framework. Gandhi's letters to Amtussalam, a Muslim girl who went on a fast in December 1946, clearly show that he does not overemphasize Amtussalam's identity as a Muslim woman. Instead she appears as as a noble Muslim soul. According to a report published in *Harijan,* it is reported: 'Certain Muslims had asked him: "Who is this Muslim woman Amtussalaam who is fasting at Sirandi?" Gandhiji said Amtussalaam had been with him for a long time. She was a true Muslim. She always had Koran-e-Sharif with her and she was never without it. She also read the Gita' (CWMG, Vol. 86, p. 373–374).

13 Bhikhu Parekh makes a very similar point. He says: 'For Gandhi, Jesus, Muhammad, Moses, and others were great spiritual explorers . . . who led exemplary lives, "discovered" some of the profoundest truths about human existence, and received a measure of divine grace at critical moments in their lives; but they were neither perfect nor Sons of God or divine emissaries. God's revelation was available to all who became worthy of it by the quality of their lives, and largely took the form of practical guidance at critical moments' (Parekh, 2001, p. 44).

14 Faisal Devji traces the placing of the Muslim past in Jinnah's political imagination. He writes: 'he imagined . . . a social contract, in which all that had been inherited from the past could be abandoned so as to begin afresh. The British Raj, therefore, had to be seen as a state of nature . . . with India and Pakistan emerging from it as if born for the first time, in a negotiated settlement that the Qaid frequently said was unprecedented in the history of nations' (Devji, 2013, pp. 97–98).

15 Reflections of this line of reasoning can also be found in Akeel Bilgrami's writings. See Bilgrami (1992, pp. 839–840).

References

Ahmad, Imtiaz (ed.). 1983. *Modernization and Social Change among Muslims in India.* New Delhi: Manohar.

Ali, Ameer Syed. 1968. Racial Characteristics of Northern India and Bengal. In Wasiti, Syed Razi (ed.), *Memoirs and Other Writings of Syed Ameer Ali.* Lahore: People Publishing House.

Banerjee, Prathama, Nigam, Aditya, and Pandey, Rakesh. 2016. The Work of Theory: Thinking across Traditions. *Economic and Political Weekly*, Vol. 51, No. 37, pp. 42–50.

Bhave, Y.G. 1997. *The Mahatma and the Muslims.* Delhi: Northern Book Centre.

Bilgrami, Akeel. 1992. What Is a Muslim? What Is a Muslim? Fundamental Commitment and Cultural Identity. *Critical Inquiry*, Vol. 18, No. 4, Identities (Summer), pp. 821–842.

Bilgrami, Akeel. 2003. Gandhi, the Philosopher. *Economic and Political Weekly*, Vol. 38, No. 39. pp. 4159–4165.

Collected Works of Mahatma Gandhi (CWMG), Vol. 18, July 1920–17 November 1920.

Collected Works of Mahatma Gandhi (CWMG), Vol. 24, May 1924–August 1924.

Collected Works of Mahatma Gandhi (CWMG), Vol. 25, August 1924–January 1925.

Collected Works of Mahatma Gandhi (CWMG), Vol. 26, January 1925–April 1925.

Collected Works of Mahatma Gandhi (CWMG), Vol. 32, November 1927–January 1927.

Collected Works of Mahatma Gandhi (CWMG), Vol. 86, 21 October 1946–20 February 1947.

Gandhi's imaginations of Muslims 71

Collected Works of Mahatma Gandhi (CWMG), Vol. 89, 01 August 1947–10 November 1947.

Devji, Faisal. 2013. *Muslim Zion: Pakistan as a Political Idea*. Cambridge, MA: Harvard University Press.

Dey, Amit. 2013. Islam and Gandhi: A Historical Perspective. *Social Scientist*, Vol. 41, No. 3/4 (March–April), pp. 19–34.

Engineer, Asghar Ali. 1975. *Islam, Muslims, India*. Bombay: Lok Vangmaya Griha.

Gandhi, M.K. 1938. *Hind Swaraj*. Ahmadabad: Navajivan Trust.

Golwalkar, M.S. 1966. *Bunch of Thought*. Bangalore: Sahitya Sindhu Prakashana.

Hasan, Mushirul. 1997. *Legacy of a Divided Nation: India's Muslims since Independence*. London: Hurst & Co.

Iqbal, Muhammad. 2006. Shikwa and Jawab-e-Shikwa. (www.columbia.edu/itc/mealac/pritchett/00urdu/iqbal/shikvah0105.html accessed on 8 August 2017).

Khilnani, Sunil. 1998. Gandhi and History. *Seminar*. Annual No. 461 (January).

Lal, Vinay. 2000. Nakedness, Nonviolence, and Brahmacharya: Gandhi's Experiments in Celibate Sexuality. *Journal of the History of Sexuality*, Vol. 9, No. 1/2 (January–April), pp. 105–136.

Madan, T.N. 2011. *Sociological Traditions: Methods and Perspectives in the Sociology of India*. Delhi: Sage.

Minault, Gail. 1982. *Khilafat Movement: Religious Symbolism and Political Mobilization in India*. New Delhi: Oxford University Press.

Mujeeb, M. 1967. *The Indian Muslims*. London: George Allen and Unwin Ltd.

Parekh, Bhikhu. 2001. *Gandhi: A Very Short Introduction*. Oxford: Oxford University Press.

Parel, Anthony J. 2007. Introduction. In Parel, Anthony J. (ed.), *Gandhi: Hind Swaraj and Other Writings*. Cambridge: Cambridge University Press, pp. 1–9.

Rudolph, Lloyd, and Rudolph, Susanne H. 2010. *Modernity of Tradition: Political Development in India*. New Delhi: Oriental Black Swan.

Strachey, John. 1894. *India*. London: Kegan Paul, Trench, Turner and Co. Ltd.

6 Gandhi, Kant and superstition

Apaar Kumar

1 Introduction

The idea that we could ferret out a universal conceptual framework on the basis of which all cultures could be evaluated was a particularly influential strand of Enlightenment thought. One consequence of this idea was that it led to the denigration of the cultures of the colonies as worthless. Many thinkers, especially in the colonies, responded to this undermining of their cultures with a 'defiant invitation to alterity or "civilisational difference"' (L. Gandhi 1998: 20). They questioned the legitimacy of the universalising grand narrative of Western modernity in evaluating their cultures. This circumstance formed one context in which Gandhi's thought was appropriated in the late-20th-century academic discourse in India. Drawing on Gandhi's critical engagement with the project of modernity, some thinkers argued that Gandhi's thought could not be assimilated to the so-called Western categories for a diverse set of reasons – because Gandhi relied on Indian thought, which is irreducible to Western thought; because he astutely saw through the pretensions of modernity from his own unique vantage point; because he Indianised Western notions beyond recognition; because he attempted to tackle the colonial/modern by employing resources available in the Indian tradition and so on.[1] This employment of Gandhi as an alternative to a colonising modernity led to important insights and remains relevant in the face of latter-day neo-colonialism. In the present context, however, one could argue, as Bernstein (1992: 65) does, that the legitimacy of the universalising grand narrative of modernity has been put in doubt, even in the Western academy. So one could contend that the emphasis should now be on a dialogue between cultures, which is of course not a new project even in the Indian context.[2]

The present chapter is a contribution to this larger project of laying out the pre-conditions of dialogue between cultures. More specifically, it raises the question of how dialogue across ideas emerging in different cultures could be established, especially in contexts that are still struggling in one way or another with the legacy of colonisation. Such a dialogue is significant, because it promises not merely to help us further understand the colonial encounter in an intellectually rigorous and balanced manner but

Gandhi, Kant and superstition 73

can potentially also lead to the emergence of norms that are, at least to some extent, generalisable across cultures. Here I explore this question regarding the possibility of dialogue between politically opposed cultures by comparing Gandhi's claim that the Bihar earthquake of 1934 should be seen as 'divine punishment' for the sin of untouchability with a similar claim in the writings of a key Enlightenment philosopher, Immanuel Kant.[3] Such an undertaking may seem odd, because we usually, with good reason, take Gandhi as a critic of the Enlightenment to be an antipode to Kant the Enlightenment figure. This may be the reason why some may believe, perhaps hastily, that any dialogue or rational comparison between Gandhi and Kant would be otiose.[4] However, as I will argue in §2, while Gandhi and Kant employ different vocabularies, and the propositional content of their respective moral psychologies differs, there are striking similarities in the manner in which they view the relationship between morality, faith, superstition and society. On the basis of this claim, in §3, I point to one way in which a dialogue between Gandhi and Kant could proceed in general, if our aim is to initiate and sustain a dialogue between two thinkers on opposite sides of the colonial divide. Establishing such a dialogue, I suggest briefly, would require seeking out broad thematic continuities between the thinkers involved with the aim of arriving at some conclusions about the themes at issue and doing so in a way that is, at least in part, generalisable across cultures.

2 Gandhi, Kant and the divine punishment argument

In the wake of the Bihar earthquake of 1934, the press quoted M. K. Gandhi as saying 'I want you, to be superstitious enough (*sic*) to believe that the earthquake is a divine chastisement for the great sin we have committed against those whom we describe as Harijans' (Bhattacharya 1997: 158). Rabindranath Tagore published an article criticising this statement by Gandhi, to which Gandhi responded with a short but rich piece of his own.[5] I begin by explicating Gandhi's defence of his statement against Tagore's criticism (§2.1) and present Kant's version of the divine punishment argument in §2.2. Finally, in §2.3, I compare the two.

2.1

Tagore offers three reasons for rejecting Gandhi's statement linking a natural disaster like an earthquake and divine punishment for a social ill (henceforth, interchangeably, 'divine punishment argument' or 'divine punishment claim'). Gandhi responds to some of Tagore's arguments and passes over others, apart from defending his own statement by means of a positive argument.

1   Tagore says that Gandhi's divine punishment argument is 'unscientific', because only physical facts can explain physical events (Ibid). Implicit

74 *Apaar Kumar*

in this argument is the mechanistic view of nature, which is characteristic of the Enlightenment. If this argument is valid, then Gandhi's drawing of a connection between the Bihar earthquake and untouchability is problematic. But Gandhi seems to deny the mechanistic view of nature when he says that it is not merely physical phenomena that 'produce' physical and spiritual consequences, but spiritual phenomena also produce physical and spiritual consequences (Ibid, 159). On the basis of this presupposition, he justifies the claim that moral actions can indeed 'produce' cosmic effects. Further, he says that this claim cannot be refuted by scientific knowledge, because science cannot give us the laws of god (Ibid, 159–60), and given our ignorance of the laws of god, what 'appears to us as catastrophes are so only because we do not know the universal laws sufficiently' (Ibid, 160). Therefore, contra the physicalist metaphysics that underlies natural science, Gandhi offers, albeit without justification, an alternative metaphysics in which spiritual and physical phenomena can reciprocally affect each other and which cannot be refuted by scientific knowledge.

2   According to Tagore, the divine punishment argument reveals the 'element of unreason . . . which is a fundamental source of all the blind powers that drive us against freedom and self-respect' for the following reasons. (a) Human nature would be superior to Godly nature if the latter needed to 'preach its lessons in good behavior in orgies of the worst possible behavior' (Ibid). (b) If morality and physical events are related, then why aren't there any earthquakes when labor is exploited in the factories? Taking (a) and (b) together, Tagore argues for the irrationality of Gandhi's position by providing a theological argument (= [a]) and pointing to an inconsistency implicit in Gandhi's position (= [b]). For his part, Gandhi does not respond individually to either (a) or (b). However, he does respond to Tagore's overall charge of irrationality. Without trying to prove that the link between the Bihar earthquake, divine punishment and untouchability is 'rational', Gandhi justifies it on the basis of an 'instinctive feeling' instead. He says that he 'instinctively feels' that the Bihar earthquake is a punishment for the sin of untouchability (Ibid, 160). This instinctive feeling cannot be proven, since it is a belief like the belief in God whose existence cannot be proven (Ibid). Here, if we bracket the merits of his argument, it is obvious that Gandhi opposes belief/faith to knowledge and instinctive feeling to reason. In his view, some combination of faith and instinctive feeling can substitute for rationality, and he goes so far as to say that Tagore's view that there is no link between physical catastrophes and moral actions can as much be categorised as 'faith' as his own opposite assertion that there is indeed such a link (Ibid, 160–61).

3   The divine punishment argument is misled in Tagore's view, because Gandhi's enemies could just as easily claim that it was Gandhi's actions

Gandhi, Kant and superstition 75

that had led to the Bihar earthquake (Ibid, 159). Gandhi does not directly respond to this standard charge against superstition – that it leads to relativism. Some Enlightenment thinkers held that values derived from universal reason could take care of such relativism and so presumed the disjunction between universal reason and relativistic superstition. Gandhi rejects the supremacy of universal reason and offers two reasons in favor of the divine punishment argument in which he also rejects superstition and appears to provide a rational justification for a 'living faith'. First, if the instinctively felt belief in the validity of the divine punishment argument leads to 'repentance and self-purification', then it could be considered beneficial even if it proves to be 'unfounded' (Ibid, 160). That is, if this belief is beneficial, it can be adopted even if it is false. This means that Gandhi does not think that the truth of the divine punishment claim can be the right measure for evaluating its significance.[6] Second, the connection between 'cosmic phenomena and human behavior' is a 'living faith', which differs from superstition. This living faith must be beneficial, but it turns into superstition if someone employs it to 'castigate' her opponents (Ibid, 160–61). Here, Gandhi's claim is that a living faith must be moral, and that the divine punishment argument instantiates this living faith because the link between the cosmic and the behavioural is drawn in the service of the eradication of untouchability. However, superstition is not admissible, since it involves castigating one's opponents, i.e., it causes dissonance in the polity.

4   In sum, Gandhi denies that the validity of the divine punishment argument can be evaluated by means of universal reason, because this argument is supported by an instinctive feeling that forms part of a living faith. This living faith differs from superstition and can bring about individual and social benefits.[7]

2.2

I now articulate (briefly) Kant's argument that natural disasters can be viewed as divine punishment. It is well-known that, for Kant, morality presupposes rationality and that the content of morality can be derived by applying the categorical imperative: an act is moral if the principle of this action can be made into a universal law. However, it is perhaps less well-known that Kant subordinates religion to morality and privileges rational faith over revealed faith (WOT, 8: 140–41; CF, 7: 28; R, 6: 136ff).[8] This rational faith requires human beings to act as if God, immortality of soul and freedom existed – what Kant calls the 'postulates' of practical reason. Kant puts the matter succinctly in his essay 'What is called orientation in thinking?'

> [R]*ational faith*, which rests on a need of reason's use with a *practical* intent, could be called a *postulate* of reason – not as if it were an insight

76   *Apaar Kumar*

which did justice to all the logical demands for certainty, but because this holding true (if only the person is morally good) is not inferior in degree to knowing, even though it is completely different from it in kind.

(8: 141–2, italics in original)

Here Kant makes a distinction between logically certain knowledge and 'holding true' (*fürwahrhalten*). In the present context, this means that if a person is moral, then she is entitled to think and act as if she were free, her soul were immortal and that God did exist.[9] This holding true is a lower-degree truth when compared to certain truth, but it is qualitatively different from the latter, primarily because it has validity merely in practical and not theoretical contexts.

Given this context, the divine punishment argument can be admitted into Kant's system only as a 'regulative idea' of this sort, that is, we are entitled to take it as true but only if our overall project is to act on the basis of morality derived out of reason. Kant says this explicitly in a set of late essays on religion, collected as *Religion within the Boundaries of Mere Reason*.

We cannot assume that the hypothesis that all evils in the world are generally to be regarded as punishments for transgressions committed was devised for the sake of a theodicy or as a contrivance for the purposes of priestly religion (cult), for it is too common to have been artificially excogitated; we must rather presume that the hypothesis is closely allied to human reason, which is inclined to link the course of nature with the laws of morality, and hence quite naturally comes up with the idea that we should seek to become better human beings first, before we can request to be freed from the ills of life, or to be compensated for them with a superior good.

(6: 74n)

So the claim that all worldly evils including natural disasters like earthquakes can be connected to our moral behavior must be viewed as somehow 'closely allied' to human reason.[10] Since this is a 'presumption' and in the service of making us act morally, we can take it as true, even though we can never know with certainty that natural and moral laws are connected.

Now, this concept of rational faith is Kant's attempt to 'deny knowledge in order to make room for faith' (CPR, Bxxx). But the problem is that if we can be allowed the postulates which are not certainly known, then we should also be allowed to believe in superstitions, miracles, grace etc. Yet Kant says that we are not entitled to the latter. I will now argue that this is not an inconsistency in Kant's philosophy to the extent that he takes our ultimate goal to be the progressive establishment of an ethical commonwealth. Taking the fulfilment of this goal as the measure, Kant distinguishes rational faith from superstition. Superstition harms the ethical community by increasing the probability of irrational actions, while rational faith does not harm but

Gandhi, Kant and superstition   77

actually fosters the establishment of an ideal moral community. I now justify this claim [(a)–(e)].

(a) Kant says that

> a pure rational faith is . . . the signpost or compass by means of which the speculative thinker orients himself in his rational excursions into the field of supersensible objects; but a human being who has common but (morally) healthy reason can mark out his path, in both a theoretical and practical respect, in a way which is fully in accord with the whole end of his vocation; and it is this rational faith which must also be taken as the ground of every other faith, and even of every revelation.
>
> (WOT, 8: 14–42)

So all faith must be rational, and revealed faith can be justified only if it is founded on rational faith. Kant exemplifies this when he re-interprets a tenet of revealed religion – the divine punishment argument – by viewing it as 'closely aligned' with human reason.

(b) Kant takes rational faith as related to the overall vocation of human beings. We can be truly moral only in an ideal ethical community. Therefore, achieving such a community should be the overarching vocation of human beings. The securing of this ideal community requires a gradual increase in legal actions and good deeds and a decrease in violence. Once a society has turned ethical as a whole, it will establish reciprocal ethical relations with other ethical societies and thus bring about what Kant calls the 'cosmopolitan society' (CF, 7: 91–92; R, Part III).

(c) If rational faith aids the human vocation of establishing an ethical commonwealth, then one way of relating morality, religion and political community in Kant's philosophy would be to say that rational faith – including the postulates but also the divine punishment argument – is useful in the formation of the ethical community. On the other hand, Kant asserts that 'impure religious ideas, which includes inner experience (enthusiasm), alleged outer experience (miracles or superstition), presumed understanding of the mysteries of the supernatural (illumination, and attempts to influence the divinity)' are not conducive to the goal of establishing such a community (R, 6: 52–53). Thus, the main criterion for deciding whether something should be considered rational faith or superstition depends on whether it serves the end of establishing an ethical community.

(d) Why does Kant think that 'impure religious ideas' detract from the establishment of the ethical commonwealth, while the postulates do not? Kant considers the idea that spiritual beings can influence nature to be impractical. Since we cannot know the nature of this influence through our senses, it would be foolhardy to act on its basis (WOT, 8:

78   *Apaar Kumar*

137–38). In contrast, Kant allows us the postulate of God, even though it cannot be sensed either. A plausible reason for this is that the postulates are meant to strengthen morality, not to produce it. One acts on the basis of the categorical imperative, because it is the rational thing to do, and the postulates can merely help strengthen our resolve to do this. Thus, in presuming a rational faith in God, we are not illegitimately presuming anything about how things are causally connected to each other in the world. We are merely employing the postulates (and the divine punishment argument) as aids in our quest for moral perfection. This is not the case with superstitions and impure religious ideas. Someone who invokes the supernatural – whether it be miracles or providing a reading of the supernatural on the basis of enthusiasm or illumination – speculates regarding a causality about which she as a human being can know nothing. If she also acts on the basis of these speculations, then she is liable to make mistakes, including the violation of her moral duties. And if she acts immorally, then she is not working towards the establishment of the moral community. Therefore, unlike the postulates, superstitions and impure religious ideas are not conducive to the formation of the ethical commonwealth.

(e) Hence, from (a)–(d), Kant links morality, religion and community in a way that allows us to distinguish superstition and rational faith. Therefore, rational faith, including the divine punishment argument, is useful in our quest to form an ideal ethical community, since it aids the achievement of moral perfection and does not rely on any false causality.

2.3

The Gandhian and Kantian versions of the divine punishment argument are similar but also different in the following ways.

(a) Gandhi makes a metaphysical claim that spiritual phenomena can produce both spiritual and physical phenomena, while Kant thinks that it is impractical to claim that spiritual beings can influence nature construed as a set of mechanical laws. However, Gandhi comes very close to Kant in his conception of the relationship between truth and the divine punishment argument. He defends his claim that the spiritual can have physical effects by saying that modern science cannot refute it, though he admits that it could be false ('unfounded'). Alternatively put, he says that the available means of achieving certain truth cannot prove the falsity of spirit causing effects in matter, although it could still be the case that this claim is false from a God's-eye perspective. This allows him to say consistently that one can instinctively feel and thus believe in the truth of the divine punishment claim, where truth is neither the truth of modern science nor truth from a God's-eye

Gandhi, Kant and superstition   79

perspective. In this Gandhi comes very close to Kant, who also denies that the practical postulates can ever be known as certain truths but admits to a notion of belief as holding something true. This leads him, as it does Gandhi, to accept the claim that one can believe in the truth of the divine punishment claim.

(b) Tagore denies any middle ground between rationality and religion, while both Gandhi and Kant seem to want to give content to this middle ground.[11] Gandhi speaks of a living faith, while Kant speaks of a rational faith. Both differ from superstition, and in both cases faith is distinguished from superstition on the basis of social criteria. For Gandhi, a living faith would turn into superstition if it were used to castigate one's enemies – that is, if it created social dissonance. For example, it would be superstition if the instinctively felt divine punishment argument were to be used to silence or harm one's political opponents. This claim presupposes that superstitious/non-superstitious beliefs relate as much to a person's attitude or world-view as to the content of these beliefs, as can be seen in the following. First, the fact that Gandhi holds that the divine punishment argument can be employed with a good conscience if the goal is the eradication of untouchability shows that those instinctively felt beliefs are acceptable that make our community more rather than less moral. So the content of non-superstitious beliefs includes all that is socially useful, and that of superstitious belief all that is socially harmful. Second, since belief in the divine punishment argument can also lead to repentance and moral upliftment, it also serves in the acquisition of the correct moral attitude.

In all of this, Gandhi's overall position broadly resembles that of Kant. Kant takes it that rational faith has no value if the agent possessing it is uninterested in morally improving herself and in contributing to the formation of an ethical commonwealth. Superstition divorces itself from morality and hinders the emergence of a perfectly ethical community.[12] Thus, for Gandhi and Kant, the criterion for the right sort of faith is ultimately this-worldly, and it is intersubjective in that faith must help all of us live a better life in a moral community.[13]

(c) One major disagreement between Gandhi and Kant relates to how they view rationality. For Kant, morality presupposes rationality, and rational faith is grounded in practical reason, and so the divine punishment argument is admissible only because it is 'closely aligned' with reason in practical (= moral) contexts. Gandhi's living faith is not based on universal reason. Rather it rests on an instinctive feeling, which can act as a premise for arguments like the divine punishment argument if the content of these arguments is practically useful for the collective. Therefore, unlike §2.3(a) and §2.3(b), one finds a genuine divergence between the views of Kant and Gandhi: the former ultimately supports the divine punishment argument on the basis of rationality (universal

80 *Apaar Kumar*

reason and holding something true), while the latter on the basis of some sort of pragmatic rationality (since the construction of an ideal society is at stake) and instinctive feeling.[14] So then, is Gandhi's instinctively felt belief consistent with Kant's holding something true? Is Gandhi's living faith so different from Kant's rational faith that there can be no possibility of dialogue?

3 Conclusion

I have suggested that Gandhi and Kant differ on the status of reason and feeling in their respective systems but share a weak notion of knowledge that allows morality and religion to be related in a way that is conducive to the achievement of an ideal ethical community. One interesting consequence of this analysis is that Tagore seems to endorse key Enlightenment ideas – mechanistic world-view, rationality as strictly universal and no middle ground between rationality and faith – in a way that differs from both Gandhi and Kant who, despite their differences, seem to possess something in common, at least on the divine punishment argument.[15] But the more important question here is that if we are committed to dialogue, how should we deal with the key difference between Gandhi and Kant on the divine punishment argument – the instinctive feeling claim in Gandhi and the reason claim in Kant? I now briefly indicate one general direction in which we could sustain a dialogue between the positions of Gandhi and Kant, despite what does seem like an insurmountable difference between them.[16]

(a) Although Gandhi speaks of instinctive feeling, he locates it within some sort of pragmatic rationality, because he thinks that this feeling can be legitimate grounds for belief and action only if it is in the service of this-worldly well-being in a moral community.[17] A similar conception of pragmatic rationality underlies Kant's acceptance of faith to the extent it can aid in the achievement of the ethical commonwealth.

(b) Living faith and rational faith are similar, since they are based on belief that is weaker than certain knowledge.

(c) If we focus on the similarities ([a]–[b]) and if we do not wish to leave the matter here but wish to iron out the differences between Gandhi and Kant on the divine punishment argument in dialogue, then we could take the following set of questions as a point of departure. Could we de-emphasise Gandhi's insistence on instinctive feeling – which makes him different from Kant – without giving up the essentials of his overall argument? If one could answer this question in the affirmative, then a Gandhian could employ the divine punishment argument to regulate her conduct, even if she rejected the claim that she instinctively feels

Gandhi, Kant and superstition   81

the validity of this argument but accepted Gandhi's characterisation of this-worldly well-being, the striving to build a just society, his notion of practical rationality etc. Similarly, could a Kantian accept the divine punishment argument even if she is not entirely convinced that the categorical imperative captures the essence of morality or that it helps us derive all our duties? If this proves to be the case, then she could bracket Kant's endorsement of universal reason and act on the basis of the other aspects of Kant's divine punishment argument – the relationship between holding something true and rational faith, the importance of working towards the ethical commonwealth etc. In addition to these questions, one could also ask if any of Gandhi's moral precepts violate the categorical imperative or if Kant's philosophy includes a notion of moral exemplarity that makes it at least comparable to Gandhi's moral philosophy in the way Bilgrami (2014: 112ff) interprets it and so on.

Needless to say, what I have offered here is merely a small part of a larger project that would require not only working through the writings of both Gandhi and Kant in a detailed manner but also working out philosophically the pre-conditions for dialogue in the post-colonial context. However, if we do decide to pursue this project of establishing a reflective conversation between Gandhi and Kant on the divine punishment argument, such an encounter between opposing thinkers (but also cultures, perspectives etc.) could well lead Gandhians and Kantians to strengthen and extend their respective views regarding the divine punishment argument. This, in turn, may engender new insights on the thorny relationship between faith, superstition and reason that might be, at least in part, generalisable across cultures. Stated more generally, this means that one way of establishing a dialogue between opposed figures from different cultures like Gandhi and Kant would be to look for broad thematic continuities between their respective philosophies with the aim of articulating something significant about some particular theme (here, the faith-superstition question) and to do so in a way that is, at least to some extent, generalisable across cultures. I am developing this claim elsewhere in the context of philosophical discussions around the notion of cultural incommensurability.

Notes

1 I do not have space to examine these positions in detail here. For the general conceptual terrain and a representative set of essays, see Raghuramaraju (2006).
2 See, for instance, Mayaram (2014) but in general also the writings of Raimon Panikkar and Ashis Nandy.
3 Kant is not the only philosopher to have addressed the relationship between natural disasters and religious and philosophical ideas. Voltaire on the 1755 Lisbon earthquake is a particularly famous example. In 'Poem on the Disaster of Lisbon'

82   *Apaar Kumar*

and later in *Candide*, Voltaire critiqued not merely Leibniz's view that ours is the best possible world but also the Christian engagement with the question of why God allows natural disasters to occur.

4 It is well-known that Gandhi was educated in the Enlightenment tradition of thought and was influenced by Western thinkers like Tolstoy and Thoreau, as well as the Bible. In addition, some commentators have tried to compare Gandhi with figures in the Western philosophical canon – for instance, Bilgrami (2014) compares Gandhi and Marx, and Sorabji (2012) compares Gandhi's thought with that of the stoics. Yet a comparison between Gandhi and Kant would seem odd to many people. Paranjape (2016) forms an exception to this general tendency. In his essay 'Kant and Gandhi: Transcivilizational Peace Perspectives', he contrasts the visions of Gandhi and Kant on peace. He argues that peace for Gandhi requires the removal of all inequalities, while, in Kant's view, inequalities cannot be removed but must be regulated in accordance with the moral law.

5 For earlier discussions of this claim, see Ramchandra Gandhi (1984: 234) who interprets Gandhi's divine punishment claim as 'insightful advaita'. Also see Ramchandra Gandhi (2015: 344–347), where this claim is interpreted in light of the theory of karma as 'moral pedagogy'. Finally, in his essay '"Natural Supernaturalism?": The Tagore-Gandhi Debate on the Bihar Earthquake', Paranjape (2016) argues that the dispute between Tagore and Gandhi on the Bihar earthquake rests on their differing views regarding how to reconcile the rational and the spiritual.

6 For Gandhi on truth, see 'Gandhi, as Philosopher' in Bilgrami (2014).

7 My aim here is to point out a set of initial resonances and differences between Gandhi and Kant on the moral significance of natural disasters. Therefore, I leave for another time a detailed discussion of Tagore's overall position on rationality and religion and the location of Gandhi's remarks on the Bihar earthquake in the context of his overall moral psychology.

8 All references to Kant are drawn from Kant (1996a) and Kant (1996b) and cited in the standard 'volume: page' format. Works by Kant are abbreviated as follows: CPR = *Critique of Pure Reason* (cited according to the standard A/B method); R = *Religion within the Boundaries of Mere Reason*; CF = *Conflict of the Faculties*; WOT = 'What Does It Mean to Orient Oneself in Thinking?'

9 Kant of course discusses the postulates in Part II of his *Critique of Practical Reason*. Since my focus here is merely on the general relationship between the postulates and rational faith, I do not discuss this section in detail here.

10 Although Kant refers to the connection between natural disasters and divine punishment in Part II of his early work 'The Only Possible Proof for a Demonstration of the Existence of God', I cite from Kant's late writings on religion (1793), because Kant rejected much in his pre-Critical writings (prior to 1781) and seriously reconsidered the question of religion in his Critical writings (1780s and 1790s).

11 For a discussion of Kant undertaken with the aim of 'reconstructing Tagore's notion of freedom' in the context of the larger Tagore-Gandhi debate, see Puri (2015: 156ff).

12 Gandhi also has a notion of Rama Rajya, which can be seen, at least prima facie, as structurally similar to Kant's ethical commonwealth, since they are both moral and teleological conceptions.

13 Broadly speaking, this interpretation of Gandhi seems prima facie to be consistent with the way Bilgrami (2014: 121) interprets Gandhi's thought. Of course, Bilgrami is not concerned with hermeneutics and, more specifically, the dialogue between cultures in the way I am here. Moreover, on Bilgrami's interpretation, Gandhi

Gandhi, Kant and superstition   83

can be seen to criticise Kant's moral philosophy to the extent his thought reflects the tension between universalisability of maxims like the categorical imperative, and Christian humility (Ibid, 113).

14 Kant speaks of the feeling of respect for the moral law, but this is entirely different from Gandhi's instinctively felt belief, which has no counterpart in Kant.

15 Here I obviously do not mean to suggest that the philosophies of Gandhi and Kant are in general more similar than that of Gandhi and Tagore (or even Nehru who is closer to Tagore than Gandhi in emphasising reason [Khilnani 2007: 96]) but only wish to point out that there is at least one significant way in which Gandhi seems closer to Kant rather than Tagore or Nehru. Minimally, this does seem to provide us with a starting point that would allow us to begin, as part of the larger dialogue between cultures, a reflective conversation between Gandhi and Kant.

16 This commitment to dialogue enabling the ironing out of differences between ideas can be viewed as a moral stance – for instance, Bernstein (1992: 65–66). I have argued elsewhere that such a commitment need not be ethical but can form part of the very structure of dialogue (see Kumar 2017).

17 I leave open what this pragmatic reasoning involves, but in general I agree with Chakrabarty (2008: 18) that Gandhi's thought cannot be understood in terms of instrumental means-ends reasoning.

References

Bernstein, Richard. 1992. *The New Constellation: The Ethical-Political Horizons of Modernity/Postmodernity*. Cambridge, MA: The MIT Press.

Bhattacharya, Sabyasachi (ed.). 1997. *The Mahatma and the Poet: Letters and Debates between Gandhi and Tagore 1915–1941*. New Delhi: National Book Trust.

Bilgrami, Akeel. 2014. *Secularism, Identity and Enchantment*. Cambridge, MA: Harvard University Press.

Chakrabarty, Dipesh. 2008. 'The Power of Superstition in Public Life in India', *Economic and Political Weekly* 43, no. 20, pp. 16–19.

Gandhi, Leela. 1998. *Postcolonial Theory: A Critical Introduction*. NSW: Allen & Unwin.

Gandhi, Ramchandra. 1984. *I Am Thou: Meditation on the Truth of India*. Pune: Indian Philosophical Quarterly Publications.

Gandhi, Ramchandra. 2015. *The Seven Sages: The Selected Essays by Ramchandra Gandhi*, ed. A. Raghuramaraju. Gurgaon: Penguin.

Kant, Immanuel. 1996a. *Practical Philosophy*, trans. and ed. Mary Gregor. Cambridge: Cambridge University Press.

Kant, Immanuel. 1996b. *Religion and Rational Theology*, trans. and ed. Allen W. Wood and George Di Giovanni. Cambridge: Cambridge University Press.

Khilnani, Sunil. 2007. 'Nehru's faith', in Anuradha Dingwaney and Rajeshwari Sunder Rajan (eds.), *The Crisis of Secularism in India*. Ranikhet: Permanent Black, pp. 89–103.

Kumar, Apaar. 2017. 'Hermeneutics From the Margins: Provisional Notes', *Trópos. Journal of Hermeneutics and Philosophical Criticism* 10, no. 1, pp. 163–183.

Mayaram, Shail (ed.). 2014. *Philosophy as Saṃvāda and Svarāj: Dialogical Meditations on Daya Krishna and Ramchandra Gandhi*. New Delhi: Sage.

Paranjape, M. 2016. *Cultural Politics in Modern India: Postcolonial Prospects, Colorful Cosmopolitanism, Global Proximities*. Oxford & New York: Routledge.

84 *Apaar Kumar*

Puri, Bindu. 2015. *The Tagore-Gandhi Debate on Matters of Truth and Untruth*. New Delhi: Springer.

Raghuramaraju, A. (ed.). 2006. *Debating Gandhi: A Reader*. New Delhi: Oxford University Press.

Sorabji, Richard. 2012. *Gandhi and the Stoics: Modern Experiments on Ancient Values*. Chicago: Chicago University Press.

7 The technology driven modern world and Gandhi

Anoop George

Introduction

Among many factors, technology remains a decisive agent of modernity. The problem of the modern epoch is a very old one. It has penetrated into our everyday life so much that it has attracted attention in a wide variety of academic disciplines and addresses different issues in literacy theory, art, architecture, social history, political theory, sociology, and philosophy (Pippin 1999: 1). What attracts our attention most is the moral crisis and the intellectual blockade propelled by the advent of modern technology and subsequently causing societies to undergo radical unwanted transformation. Philosophically speaking, modernity is that self-understanding whereby humans understand themselves as subjects separated from objects, as Descartes formulated in his distinction between *res extensa* and *res cogitans*.[1] Technological progress and scientific advancements continue to be the greatest accomplishments of modern civilizations. While we celebrate such endeavours, none can forget the rot that lies dormant in it. While everyone takes recourse to technology, the evil it perpetrates has been a serious concern for many philosophers, and the most important aspect in question is what it is to be a human subject, especially the kind that the modern societies aspire to. Though there emerged a new philosophy during the time of Francis Bacon and Descartes, which indeed triggered enlightenment and progress, it turned out to manifest the 'death of God' or nihilism in the 19th and early 20th centuries, especially in the interpretation of Nietzsche[2] and Heidegger, with a distinctive focus on the rise of modernity and technological progress. Nietzsche and Heidegger and a host of others, Gandhi prominent among them, considered degradation of values undisputedly inherent in technological advancements. The disenchantment with the modern notion of progress, which according to the critics comes either with a sense of nihilism or an elevation of man to a superman (Pippin 1999: 2). The primacy of Gandhi lies in the fact that he is one among many thinkers of 20th century who valued technology to great heights but always remained anxious of its effects on the unreflective humans in whose discretion they are finally adhered. Gandhi, like many other critics, was dissatisfied with modernity because it

86   *Anoop George*

failed to deliver what it had promised. In Gandhi's view the modern tech-nological civilization denudes the human interior dimension and destroys the essence of the soul. Gandhi's preoccupation was the inner individual. But there would be no sense to the inside without the outside as long as one bodily exists. Hence the outside world, which is technologically modernised, needs to be understood and meaningfully appreciated. Gandhi believes that the modern technology is harmful because human beings are unable to put a check or find a middle path in their engagement with technology. I shall now discuss the Gandhian views of a technologically driven modern world with a philosophical exposition of technology and technological reduction-ism. I will also discuss the Gandhian vision of Indian economy within the framework of modern Western technology.

Modernity and Gandhi

Though we are quick to cherish the musings of modernity, the uncontrolled production, relentless modification and further innovation of technology and a subsequent growth of modern industrial societies create more decadence among human beings than they intended to have solved. We tend to call ourselves modern when we construct mammoth concrete structures, pollut-ing even the smallest rivers that are around, jamming every road, destroying natural habitats of millions of creatures, even causing their extinction, and finally we ourselves become totally self-centered, individualistic, and discon-tented. The growing concern expressed by the critics of technology such as Martin Heidegger, Herbert Marcuse, and Hannah Arendt,[3] to name a few, clearly shows the need of addressing these issues and the violence inherent in the modern technologies towards both the animate and inanimate environ-ment. Gandhi's interpretation of technological modernity has a much wider impact. He focused more on the degradation of human values, morality, and integrity. He preached about the primacy of the 'spiritual' and the impor-tance of individuals turning inward to find the real purpose of existence. The real danger lies in the fact that we are discontented with everything, and we tend to believe that we will be satisfied when we have material progress in abundance. Gandhi argues that 'An ant is perfect, because it does not wish to become better. But we have got to progress' (Gandhi, *Collected Works*, vol. 61, p. 580). The sense of progress has culminated in what we call today the modern. It is characterised by such features as rationalism, secularisation, industrialisation, scientific culture, individualism, technological mastery of nature, the drive towards globalisation, and liberal democracy (Parekh 2001: 78). Philosophers like Heidegger would consider modernity to be an ontol-ogy that captures the modern human imagination so absolutely that it is difficult to see how one can get out of it. Heidegger for sure believes that the enticingly oppressive tendency of the ontology of the modern age thereby has entered a phase of decadence and loss. It is not the recovery of moder-nity's moral sources that Heidegger visualises but its complete transformative rejection – a new revealing of Being or truth. Gandhi conceived that every civilization was inspired by a distinct conception of human beings who always wanted a break from the past. But most of the time this distinct conception was mistaken and finally ended up resulting evil. According to Gandhi this was the case with modern civilization as well. Although it had many achievements to its credit, it was fundamentally flawed, as is evident in the fact that it is aggressive, imperialistic, violent, exploitative, brutal, unhappy, restless, and devoid of a sense of direction and purpose. Gandhi thought that this was because modern civilization neglected the primacy of the soul and privileged the body and the pleasures that were intended with it, further misunderstood the nature and the limits of reason, and had no appreciation for the nuances of individuality (Parekh 2001: 79).

Gandhi contended that modernity backed by luring technology had encaged the individual within herself and elicited individualism. An individual loses her authentic identity in individualism. According to Charles Taylor, individualism is the first of three malaises of modernity. Taylor fears that individualism would result as 'people come to see themselves more and more atomistically, as less and less bound to their fellow citizens in common projects and allegiances' (Taylor 1995: 282). Gandhi strongly contends that the danger of individualism or atomism begins with man's extreme preoccupation with the body. Once man's entire preoccupation is turned towards the body his focus will be dominated by the appetitive instinct, and what remains will be unrestrained satisfaction of wants, which would eliminate everything of moral depth. The appetitive instinct, on its part, would trigger a materialistic stand, which again further triggers a capitalistic economy and the accumulation of wealth in the hands of a few. On a philosophical stand, Gandhi argues that every individual should understand that she is a rational entity and has been thrown into a world of meaning and culture. Self-disclosure happens with and through our temporal, linguistic embeddedness in the world. But the danger erupts when the entire preoccupation is geared towards the body and neglects the interior dimension.

Gandhi believes that invention of various machineries helped man to take up difficult tasks and accomplish great heights. Machines also created leisure and increased human efficiency, and above all it was indispensable when the labour flock was scarce. His greater concern would be that the machineries should function within a well-established moral theory to guide how an individual should conduct herself in a society with well sounding inter-personal and intra-personal relations. The modern individualism propelled by the overhauling technology has made us so self-centered that we see everything, even other human beings, merely as a means for exploitation and of use value. This mostly happens because we live and work without a fundamental ontology and with no regard for wider moral and cultural supremacy. The crisis of modern technology is that the machineries were introduced when there was no obvious need for them and with a certainty that thousands

88 *Anoop George*

would be thrown out of work, and this is what Gandhi calls a craze for machinery. He argues:

> What I object to, is the *craze* for machinery, not machinery as such. The craze is for what they call labour-saving machinery. Men go on 'saving labour' till thousands are without work and thrown on the open streets to die of starvation. I want to save time and labour, not for a fraction of mankind, but for all. I want the concentration of wealth, not in the hands of the few, but in the hands of all. Today machinery merely helps a few to ride on the backs of millions. The impetus behind it all is not the philanthropy to save labour, but greed. It is against this constitution of things that I am fighting with all my might.
>
> (Gandhi, *Collected Works*, vol. 25, p. 251)

Gandhi envisioned that once we were totally technicised there would be no one to guard the inexorable momentum of technology, and gradually its unbridled growth would reduce human beings into hapless victims of it and open up a new form of slavery. In such a scenario what suffers most is the moral life of the individual. When profit becomes the sole end of life, exploitation of other humans will be unavoidable. Morality becomes as abstract as the human being herself. Morality was seen not as an expression of human dignity but as a restriction of freedom, a kind of tax one had to pay in order to be able to enjoy one's residual freedom unhindered. It was therefore reduced to the barest minimum, requiring a little more than what was needed to prevent people from harming or destroying each other. In Gandhi's view only a moral agent could stand against jealousy, hatred, callousness, ill-will, sordid thoughts, and fantasies. But since we are blinded by our obsessive preoccupations with the worldly things, the modern man finds it insignificant to maintain the purity of the self. Hence the ideal modern man could finally be aggressive, ambitious, and a self-centred person (Parekh 2001: 80). Gandhi in all his attempts painstakingly tries to retrieve the authenticity of man by emphasising the primacy of the inner spiritual self, which is beyond all forms of corruption. The greatest danger of modern technology on humans, as Gandhi envisioned, is the technological reductionism itself.

Technological reductionism

While accepting various aspects of technology and scientific temper, what remained a serious concern for Gandhi was technological reductionism. Technological reductionism is a process in which, with the advent technology, there exists a sense of loss of value. Gandhi envisioned that a technology-driven modern world is reductive in nature. A reductive approach disentangles phenomena from their rich horizon of meaning and is averse to the ambiguity wrought by a rich context of significance. A reductive approach

Modern world and Gandhi   89

usually overlooks the rich cultural layers that pins communities together. For Gandhi it is much more severe; it destroys peace and harmony and it implicitly upholds violence. Reductionism, says Richard Jones, makes us believe that 'what is apparently real is ultimately "nothing but" something else – either its parts or something that is more basic' (Jones 2000: 13). Thus in reductionism one form of reality is reduced to another form with the aim of grasping it fully and disengaging it from its context and horizon of significance. Gandhi envisioned technological reductionism to be a serious predicament, especially among the youth of the Indian society. Gandhi upholds that once technological reductionism creeps into our life then what remains will be meaninglessness. The end point of reductionism is exploitation of oneself, nature, and other human beings. In the modern times reductionism is the effect of the scientific-technological civilization. Reductionist thinking reminds us that whatever is really real is only the physical, the rational, the programmable, the formulaic, and the quantifiable.

Reductionism exposes the 'for-ness' of things: things exist for our manipulation, use, and optimisation and that alone. The cultural layers around a thing, which give it significance and import, are thus disparaged. Instead, modern ways of dealing with things would mean exploitation and manipulation. Reductionism converts all our comportments towards things utility-oriented so that we tacitly understand them always already as standing reserve. Layers of meaning dissuade us usually from this project of reduction, and hence they are to be denigrated, ignored, and made to disappear from our horizon. For Gandhi, this is the primary way of becoming the modern self. According to him this form of the modern self is too materialistic and would eventually destroy every society.

A lecture that Gandhi delivered at the Muir College Economic Society in Allahabad, after his return from South Africa, shows his views on the dangers of modern materialism and a subsequent destruction of societies. This is what he argues in the lecture titled 'Does Economic Progress Clash with Real Progress?':

> This land of ours was once, we are told, the abode of the gods. It is not possible to conceive gods inhabiting a land which is made hideous by the smoke and the din of mill chimneys and factories and whose roadways are traversed by rushing engines dragging numerous cars crowded with men mostly who know not what they are after, who are often absent-minded, and whose tempers do not improve by being uncomfortably packed like sardines in boxes and finding themselves in the midst of utter strangers who would oust them if they could and whom they would in their turn oust similarly. I refer to these things because they are held to be symbolical of material progress. But they add not an atom to our happiness.

> (Gandhi, *Collected Works*, vol. 13, p. 315)

90   *Anoop George*

A technologically driven modern world is what is most appealing to all. What is the use if we all live in a highly modernised world with no room for morality? In the modern world 'factories have risen on the corpses of men, women and children, how as the country has rapidly advanced in riches, it has gone down in morality' (Ibid). When a society is constructed without the trace of morality, it will be like a builder building a house on the sand, which will have a terrible fall when difficult days arrive. When morality disappears, then the so-called progress will be left with adulteration, bribery, exploitation, life-destroying trades, insanitation, deaths, alcoholism, etc. According to Gandhi a civilization is not a merely mushrooming of concrete structures or when a certain section of a society grows rich; rather he argues:

> Civilization is that mode of conduct which points out to man the path of duty. Performance of duty and observance of morality are convertible terms. To observe morality is to attain mastery over our mind and our passions. So, doing, we know ourselves. The Gujarati equivalent for civilisation means 'good conduct'. If this definition be correct, then India, as so many writers have shown, has nothing to learn from anybody else, and this is as it should be. We notice that mind is a restless bird; the more it gets the more it wants, and still remains unsatisfied. The more we indulge our passions, the more unbridled they become. Our ancestors, therefore, set a limit to our indulgences. They saw that happiness was largely a mental condition. A man is not necessarily happy because he is rich or unhappy because he is poor. The rich are often seen to be unhappy, the poor to be happy. Millions will always remain poor. Observing all this, our ancestors dissuaded us from luxuries and pleasures.
>
> (Gandhi 2009: 67–68)

Gandhi appreciates the Indian culture and goes to the extent of saying that we have everything to become a civilised society. Gandhi argues that the moral ideals of Ahimsa or non-violence cannot be practiced in a world that is blinded by the charms of modernity and machine technology. In the modern times there is no fulfillment even in new inventions since every invention triggers mass production and lacks novelty. Gandhi gives the interesting example of the Singer sewing machine to show how inventions and the modern machine craze can be looked at in a different way. About the Singer sewing machine, Gandhi says that it is one of the few useful things ever invented, and there is a romance about the device itself. Singer saw his wife labouring over the tedious process of sewing and seaming with her own hands, and simply out of his love for her, he devised the sewing machine, in order to save her from unnecessary labour. He, however, saved not only her labour but also the labour of everyone who could purchase a sewing machine. In a technologically driven modern world, inventions are merely for the sake of mass production. There

Modern world and Gandhi 91

is neither love in production nor in what is produced. Gandhi clearly makes the distinction between invention and invention. He argues that we should

> prize every invention of science made for the benefit of all. There is a difference between invention and invention. I should not care for the asphyxiating gases capable of killing masses of men at a time. The heavy machinery for work of public utility which cannot be undertaken by human labour has its inevitable place, but all that would be owned by the State and used entirely for the benefit of the people. I can have no consideration for machinery which is meant either to enrich the few at the expense of the many, or without cause to displace the useful labour of many.
>
> (Gandhi, *Collected Works*, vol. 61, p. 187)

Gandhi's apprehension towards machinery was that finally machinery would be in the hands of a few powerful people who would use it for large scale industrialisation and which would result in unemployment, poverty, and the death of many. The advent of technological modernity continues to haunt the modern man because it overshadows our essence as 'openness' to truth. But the danger lies in the fact that the modern man, mesmerised by the allurement of technological modernity, has failed to be reflective and acts immorally. Not thinking and sinking deeper into technological reductionism makes us gather and bring to the fore stranger and stranger objects like the atomic bomb, which could annihilate the planet and humanity. This could mean that we gradually close up other meaningful possibilities of the disclosure of phenomena. Gandhi terms this as the selfishness of the modern man whose only preoccupation is profit making at any cost.

In the next section I will take forward this modern technological reductive approach towards understanding the economic progress as envisioned by Gandhi in British India. I will deal mostly with the ideal of *swadeshi* to explicate the Gandhian economic vision and technology.

Gandhi's economic vision and technology

Mahatma Gandhi was not a conventional economist. His views on economics largely originated with his own vision of impoverished India following his extensive travels across the country after his return to India from South Africa. The British rule had devastated the Indian economy. India merely became a producer of raw materials for the heavy industries of England and a marketplace for its finished products. The depleting economy and introduction of Western machinery made Gandhi invent, as always experimenting and evolving, measures to rejuvenate the Indian economy and impoverishment. He advocated *swaraj* and *swadeshi* for *sarvodaya*.

92   Anoop George

Swaraj for Gandhi was not merely freedom from the British rule but rather a vision of the self-dignity, self-reliance, and self-sustenance. Since the majority of Indians at that time lived in villages it was also quite necessary for Gandhi to design a *swadeshi* movement, which refers to equal concern and *swaraj* in the mundane life for the welfare for all – *sarvodaya*. It meant social consciousness above self-interest with inherent self-sacrifice. It is a dynamic philosophy to decolonise the mindset of consumer economics to reconstruct a welfare society.

One indispensable aspect of any Gandhian initiative was the inclusion of strict ethical framework. According to Gandhi, economics without ethics cannot sensibly exist. He argues that, 'If dharma and economic interests cannot be reconciled, either the conception of that dharma is false or the economic interest takes the form of unmitigated selfishness and does not aim at collective welfare' (Gandhi, *Collected Works*, vol. 31, p. 276). He believed in normative science with inherent morality, more humane and not ego-driven self-interest. A strong sense of spirituality and most primarily the purity of intention is what remained summum bonum for Gandhi.

Gandhi's opposition to technology was not because he disliked technology but rather, according to him, technology was dehumanising; it is against equality in terms of economics and opportunity. He was discontented with technology because it rendered joblessness. 'I am against machines just because they deprive men of their employment and render them jobless. I oppose them not because they are machines but because they create unemployment' (Gandhi, *Collected Works*, vol. 87, p. 326). Gandhi knew that the number of educated young people in India was increasing and that they needed jobs. A total mechanisation of India would certainly throw a vast number of people out of jobs. Unemployment in a country like India would be horrendous as it would lead to many social evils.

Swadeshi was Gandhi's important economic imaginings. It depicts what is made in one's own land. Gandhi envisioned that embracing *swadeshi* was the sole remedy to address issues like clothing, hunger, and much of the agricultural and economic problems of the country and also to arrest the economic hegemony of the British raj. *Swadeshi* was programmed to make every Indian village self-supporting and self-producing. Gandhi went to the extent of saying that 'It is through swadeshi that we shall get swaraj' (Gandhi, *Collected Works*, vol. 16, p. 18). Being true to the spirit of *swadeshi*, Gandhi says that we need to shun the machine-made products of the British and focus more on small-scale industries in the villages, like weaving, that are more convenient for people to manage and use. Large-scale industries will require much space and logistics to install the machines, while the cottage industries are simple and require minimum effort to handle. Gandhi argues that

> hand-weaving seems very easy, for it does not require all this effort. A man of average ability can learn the work in six months' time and one

Modern world and Gandhi   93

with some intelligence can pick it up in three months. The method of
making yarn is altogether simple. I took no more than 15 days to learn it.
(Ibid, p. 21)

Modern technology has its own drawbacks. Gandhi's contention towards
technology was that it takes away our labour from us, and in return it makes
us lazy and lethargic. Gandhi argues that even before the invention of weaving machines we produced cloth. According to him every household in India
knew how to produce cloth (Ibid). But gradually, with the arrival of machinery, ease and comfort penetrated into our lives, and it swiftly deprived us of
our own skills, creative art, and labour.

Industrial development certainly benefits a society with large scale
production to meet the requirements of a huge population. While many
considered industrialisation as an option for India, Gandhi vehemently
opposed it. Adoption of machinery for economic stability was a myth for
Gandhi believing that a nation does not progress when there is surplus
production. Technological growth is unlimited and ever expanding, and it
has a dynamic of its own, which knows no bounds (Dasgupta 1993: 148).
Gandhi argued that the modernised life of the West is highly artificial and
has grown quickly but without room for thought for long term sustainabil-
ity. Modern technology has not brought equality or economic stability. It
has caused materialism and consumerism and divided the humans into rich
and poor. Gandhi has an interesting reply to the mass production promised
by the modern industries. Mass production in essence should be the production by 'masses' for the 'masses', but on the contrary modern machines
guarantee employment for a few people and not the masses. Gandhi argues
that the spinning-wheel, on the other hand, guarantees mass production
and mass production in people's own homes (Gandhi, *Collected Works*,
vol. 48, p. 166). Gandhi would ask 'if you multiply individual production
to millions of times, would it not give you mass production in tremendous
scale?' (Ibid).

The important part of Gandhi's economic aspiration is to meet each one's
need and not anyone's greed. Machines do help us to add leisure and ease
in our work, but if we do not put a check on them it will enslave us. He
argues, 'I am not against machinery as such but I am totally opposed to it
when it masters us' (Gandhi, *Collected Works*, vol. 64, p. 118). Machinery
should be used where it is benefitting human health and welfare, communication, and information without compromising our indigenous skills and
village economics; handicraft and cottage industries could go along with
the technological advances, preserving our cultural heritage, values, and
art. Introducing certain machines in the villages may harm the villagers by
depriving them of their employment and polluting the environment. What is
most admirable about Gandhi is his emphasis on self-reliance and dedication
for hard work. Economic stability of a nation can be envisaged if everyone
in the country begins to work hard. His contention towards technology was

94 *Anoop George*

mostly because it deprives us of our hard work and has made us lazy. He even goes to the extent of saying that we should not freely feed able-bodied poor as this will deprive them of their desire for hard work (Gandhi, *Collected Works*, vol. 21, p. 167).

However modern economists might say that the Gandhian economic ideals were utopian in nature and have failed in practise, but proposing an economic method in the first half of the 20th century would not have been easy for Gandhi with poverty and famine on one side and the mighty unshakable British raj on the other. Nevertheless his will to arrest the booming Western technological machinery with the introduction of *swadeshi*, which again in turn would change the course of Indian economy, is a remarkable one. His imaginative idea of charkha making Khadi turned into a movement with a clear message of self-reliance, *swadeshi*, and economics. The progress of Khadi, he believed, does not depend upon the ups and downs of the market. It depends upon the purity of our transactions (Gandhi, *Collected Works*, vol. 80, p. 252).

Gandhi's economic philosophy is aimed at balanced growth and social justice and solutions to social problems due to inequality – including violence – and to promise a quality of life to all, leaving no one. There are revival efforts of traditional weaving as a source of livelihood and women empowerment. Gandhi's concerns are globally recognised and are part of discourse at different levels to address human failings. As universalist as he was in approach, his thoughts need interpretation in the present-day context of globalisation.

Conclusion

Gandhi's attempt was to recover the lost ground and meaning for modern humans. Though he overlooked certain important aspects of modernity and modern technology, he is right in saying that it has the tendency to dehumanise. The technologically driven modern world and the civilization that followed are the greatest achievements of the modern man. The disillusionment about the modernity is that its key imagination continues to hold a disengaged, autonomous, and atomistic self, which is empowered for a moral failure and hence a total destruction. In Gandhi's understanding the modern mechanised human being is a pure rational self. And vice versa, a pure rational self has historically assisted moderns to usher in the age of science and technology, productive systems, and market economy. Gandhi is ever remembered as the chief exponent of India's freedom struggle. His struggle was not only against the British but also against Western culture, which he feared would engulf the Indian culture. He devised the methods of *satyagraha*, *sarvodaya*, and *swadeshi* to counter social, political, and economic wrongs, and that made him a unique politician. What troubled Gandhi with regard to technology and technological modernity was the loss of human dignity and morality. Gandhi's own life was a message to those who

Modern world and Gandhi   95

embraced modernity unreflectively. In his ashram he gathered together like-minded people whose pursuit was to seek Truth or God and uphold morality. Gandhi feared that technology and technological reductionism would wipe away many hallowed principles of our culture. Modernisation and mechanisation have caused deforestation and environmental degradation. There is depletion of resources and pollution, socioeconomic inequality, and discontentment. The future is expected to have more technology from the innovative human mind. We need to re-affirm our cultural values and morality in the body of technology to become more useful without subverting human values. Morality, which was central to Gandhi's ideals and principles, is yet relevant, notwithstanding the changing present-day realities.

Notes

1 Rene Descartes (1596–1650) is famously known for the statement 'I think therefore I am'. This assertion had a great influence on the Cartesian dualism or the mind-body problem. While Descartes uses the term *res cogitans* to mean an exclusive intellectual independence from the body, he uses *res extensa* to mean an 'extended and unthinking thing'.
2 Friedrich Nietzsche (1844–1900) was a German philosopher and a cultural critic. Nietzsche is well known for the statement 'Death of God', which occurs in several of his works, most notably in *The Gay Science* (for more details see Nietzsche, F. 2001. *The Gay Science*. Bernard Williams (ed.), Josefine Nauckhoff (Trans.). Cambridge: Cambridge University Press.
3 Martin Heidegger (1889–1976) was one of the most influential philosophers of the 20th century who contributed towards philosophy of technology. Herbert Marcuse (1898–1979) and Hannah Arendt (1906–1975) were students of Heidegger and were influential critics of modern technology. Heidegger contends that modern technology differs from the previous technologies primarily because it 'enframes' everything around it. The danger of enframing is that it leaves every reality as 'standing reserve' for human manipulation. Herbert Marcuse is known for his idea of 'technological rationality', proposed in his 1941 article 'Some Social Implications on Modern Technology'. Marcuse argues that the advent of technology can alter our rational decisions and can change what is considered as rational within a society (for more details please see Marcuse, Herbert. 1941. 'Some Social Implications of Modern Technology', in *Studies in Philosophy and Social Sciences*, 9(3): 414–439). Hannah Arendt analyses the human activity in terms of labour, work, and action, which furnishes a holistic critique of the modern technoscience. According to her, modern technology disrupts our performative relationship with the natural world. (Please see Arendt, H. 1998. *The Human Condition* (Second ed.). Chicago: University of Chicago Press.)

References

The Collected Works of Mahatma Gandhi. Vols. 1–100. New Delhi: Publications Division, (1958–1994).
Dasgupta, A. K. 1993. *A History of Indian Economic Thought*. London: Routledge Publishers.
Gandhi, M. K. 2009. *Hind Swaraj and Other Writings*, ed. Anthony J. Parel. Cambridge: Cambridge University Press.

96 Anoop George

Jones, R. H. 2000. *Reductionism: Analysis and the Fullness of Reality*. Cranbury: Associated University Press.

Parekh, B. 2001. *Gandhi: A Very Short Introduction*. New York: Oxford University Press.

Pippin, R. B. 1999. *Modernism as a Philosophical Problem*. Oxford: Blackwell Publishers.

Taylor, C. 1995. *Philosophical Arguments*. Cambridge: Harvard University Press.

8 Negotiating differences in a Gandhian way

Ahimsa, love, compassion and the gift of fearlessness

Bindu Puri

It is difficult to limit a discussion on the contemporary relevance of the Gandhian legacy to one central point because many things Gandhi said and did remain important to our contemporary predicaments. Nevertheless, if one is to locate a central point of contemporary relevance in the Gandhian legacy one could make a philosophically compelling case for Gandhian *ahimsa*/non-violence. The *ahimsanat*/non-violent Gandhian response to the 'otherness' of the different – frequently hostile – 'other' seems especially significant given that the contemporary world is both plural and conflict-ridden. It is also possible to argue that Gandhian *ahimsa* provides an alternative to both liberal tolerance and non-liberal conflict and violence as ways of responding to different 'others'. These last two are of course the more characteristic ways of responding to difference in the contemporary world. One is commonly either a liberal responding to difference with tolerance (coming from a scepticism about all truth claims) or one is simply non-liberal responding to different 'others' with conflict and often violence. The contemporary relevance of the Gandhian alternative as *ahimsa* and the gift of fearlessness to all different and differing others is apparent enough. Difference can of course be along many lines – gender, race, religion, ethnic origin, language or culture. Yet it almost always presents itself as an 'otherness' from oneself or one's group that needs to be overcome.

Gandhi was no stranger to conflicts with different 'others' and had himself dealt with three fairly significant self and 'other' conflicts – with the racial, colonial and religious 'others'. It was perhaps in response to such conflicts that Gandhi had developed his own insights into the connection between truth and *ahimsa* and thought out a proper/rightful response to difference. The Gandhian response was permeated by non-violence in the interest of arriving at truth. One can think of Gandhian *satyagraha* as the practise of *ahimsa*/non-violence in the interest of arriving at the truth between two opposing positions.

Having spelt out the central Gandhian legacy, one needs to philosophically engage with what is distinctive about this *ahimsanat* response to difference and to conflicts that can emerge from difference. This chapter will make an attempt to make such an engagement across three sections. The first section

98   *Bindu Puri*

will explore the idea of *ahimsa* in Gandhi. It is often argued that Gandhian *ahimsa* was much more than merely non-injury. Gandhi conveyed what he understood by *ahimsa* by using a host of other related terms. In this connection, the section entitled '*Ahimsa*: to own kinship with those most distant from oneself' will explore the terms that Gandhi had invoked in connection with *ahimsa-swabhava*,[1] kinship, love, compassion and the gift of fearlessness to all. One would not be able to get a sense of what was philosophically significant about Gandhian *ahimsa* without building in its intimate connection with truth. The second section of this chapter, '*Ahimsa* and *satya*',[2] will bring out the significance of this connection to a proper understanding of Gandhi's response to different 'others'. The third section of the chapter is entitled 'To tolerate or to honour: liberalism and Gandhi'. This section will bring out the differences between Gandhi's position on treating hostile others with love (born of unflinching belief in absolute equality) and the liberal position on tolerance. The conclusion to the chapter will recapitulate the different strands in the argument.

Ahimsa: to own kinship with those most distant from oneself

One of the most fascinating metaphors that Gandhi used to convey his understanding of *ahimsa* was that of owning 'kinship with not merely the ape but the horse and the sheep, the lion and the leopard, the snake and the scorpion' (Gandhi, *eCWMG*, vol. 36: 5). In a set of two interesting essays written in *Young India* in 1926 on the *swabhava*/nature/*own most orientation of man*, Gandhi had explained that owning kinship with the most distant/different 'others' was *ahimsa* and that such *ahimsa* was man's *swabhava* and his special virtue/*khaaslakshana*. In this set of essays Gandhi went on to write that

> the difficult dharma which rule my life, and I hold ought to rule that of every man and woman, impose this unilateral obligation (*ekpakshi farj*) on us. And it is so imposed because only the human is the image of God.
> (Gandhi, *eCWMG*, Vol. 36: 5)

Quite clearly Gandhi was using the idea of man's *swabhava*/*innermost nature or orientation* as being constituted by the unilateral obligation to own kinship with the snake, the scorpion, etc. as a metaphor. The point was perhaps to draw attention to man's *unilateral* obligation *qua* man towards the 'otherness' of the 'other' different from the self. Such a sense of *farj*/obligation to the other is perhaps thought of most easily by the almost instinctive individual sense of what is owed to one's family members, and so Gandhi invoked the idea of kinship in this context. This idea of *ahimsa* as the unilateral obligation to respond to a hostile other, as one would respond to one's own kith and kin, was also invoked much earlier in *Hind Swaraj*. Gandhi had spoken of *ahimsa*/non-violence in the context of dealing with a

Negotiating differences in a Gandhian way   99

thief as a hostile and armed 'other' in one's own home. He had recommended treating the thief with *ahimsa* as if he was a kin in fact as 'an ignorant brother' (Gandhi in Parel, 2009: 81). In both ordinary life and conceptual discussion, the idea of kinship is strongly associated with love. Gandhi also invoked both kinship and the associated idea of love to think out the meaning of *ahimsa*. It is interesting that Gandhi most often spoke of love/*prem* in connection with non-violence/*ahimsa*. He explained that the sort of love he had in mind was a love of those who differed from oneself. Gandhi said:

> It is no non-violence if we merely love those who that love us [sic]. It is non-violence only when we love those that hate us.
>
> (Bose, 1948: 17)

This Gandhian idea of loving those who differ from oneself and even loving those who hate oneself makes it apparent that Gandhian *ahimsa* as love should not be confused with romantic love. Gandhi's use of love in connection with *ahimsa* seems to refer instead to a universal/detached love of all human and non-human 'others'. What Gandhi seemed to have meant by *ahimsa* was a sort of non-passionate love that transforms both the giver and the receiver. Gandhi had credited Patanjali as the source of this notion of love as transformative – '*Ahimsa pratishtaya tat sathir dhover atyaga*' 'Hate Dissolves in the presence of Love' (Patañjali yogadarshanam ii.35) (Gandhi, *eCWMG*, Vol. 48: 327).

Gandhian *ahimsa* involved the practice of non-violence as a unilateral obligation to love 'others' without passion and to own kinship with them. One can perhaps understand what is meant by kinship with different 'others' – to love them as one would one's own kin – by bringing in another term that Gandhi invoked to think *ahimsa*. This was the idea of compassion or *daya*. Gandhi's mentor and guide, the Jain thinker Raychandbhai Mehta (whom Gandhi had first met in 1891), had emphatically emphasised *dayadharma*/the duty of compassion. The second chapter in Raychandbhai's book *Mokshamala* (which we know that he had asked Gandhi to read) was titled 'A religion accepted by all' (*sarvamanya Dharma*). This chapter identified the essence of religion as *daya*/compassion and called for compassion to all living beings. Following Raychandbhai, Gandhi also often invoked *daya* in connection with *ahimsa*. For example, in Chapter XVII of *Hind Swaraj*, quoting the poet Tulsidas, Gandhi had said:

> The force of compassion – that is the force of love, that is satyagraha.
>
> (Gandhi in Parel, 2009: 88)

Raychandbhai had argued that compassion can be best practised through *abhaydaan* or the gift of fearlessness to all life and that this gift of fearlessness is realised only through taking a vow of non-violence. On his view, non-violence was in fact the primary vow required to practise *daya*/compassion.

100 *Bindu Puri*

Both Raychandbhai and Gandhi clearly emphasised the intimate inter-relationship between non-violence compassion and gifting fearlessness to all 'others'.

According to Gandhi, a non-violent and good human life involved all four concepts – non-violence, love, compassion and gifting fearlessness to all human and non-human 'others'. Gandhi argued, for instance, that *daya*/compassion towards the differing, hostile 'other' was directly involved in confronting his/her hostility by non-violent resistance rather than violence. Gandhi connected such compassion to *abhaydaan* or the unconditional gift of fearlessness to all beings. He argued that such a gift was also the requisite of true religion:

> Fearlessness is the first requisite of true religion.
> (Gandhi, *eCWMG*, Vol. 24: 411)

One can philosophically reinterpret the connection Gandhi made between compassion and the gift of fearlessness if one thinks about what might be involved in cultivating the attitude of compassion towards all beings. Feeling compassion for another seems to involve empathy towards that other, and, more than empathy, it involves an empathetic identification with the other. Clearly one can only feel compassion for different 'others' – including threatening religious others or politically hostile unjust others – when one does not fear their 'otherness'. If the difference of others makes one full of fear, one cannot empathetically identify with them. It seems possible to argue that some sort of empathetic identification seems to be essential to feeling compassionate towards another. For instance, one feels compassion for a grieving person because at some level one can identify with the experience of his/her loneliness or loss. Think also of the compassion one feels towards the pain of the ill or the bereaved. One identifies with their experiences because they are inalienable parts of the human condition. When one fears the other, one is immediately distanced from that other. In such a case one certainly cannot identify with that other, and consequently her pain does not evoke compassion in one's heart. It follows that one can argue that it is only when one feels fearless when confronted by hostile 'others' that one can identify with and feel compassionate towards them. Once one is fearless and full of compassion one also makes such hostile 'others' feel fearless towards oneself. Gandhi thought that the good human life essentially involved such a gift of fearlessness towards all others by becoming fearless oneself:

> In its positive form ahimsa means the largest love, the greatest charity. . . . 'Gift of life' is the greatest of all gifts. A man who gives it in reality disarms all hostility. He has paved the way to an honourable understanding. And none who is himself subject to fear can bestow that gift. He must therefore be himself fearless.
> (Gandhi in Murti, 1970: 137)

Negotiating differences in a Gandhian way 101

Gandhi seemed to have connected this 'gift' of life/fearlessness to others with two other related dispositions – the ability to forget and to forgive. Gandhi spoke of the need to inculcate both abilities as part of developing an *ahimsanat*/non-violent disposition of character. It seems fairly easy to understand why Gandhi should have connected the ability to forgive with *ahimsa*. For it seems apparent enough that if one is not able to forgive the 'other' for what one thinks are injuries to oneself there can be no feeling of non-violence, much less love, for the erring other. Yet Gandhi thought that even the memory of past injuries to oneself (or one's own group) needed to be forgotten before one could feel that the other was like 'one's own'. In this connection it is important to note that in *Hind Swaraj*, the editor had emphasised the importance of forgetting:

> The Hindus and the Mahomedans have quarrelled. An ordinary man will ask them to forget all about it, he will tell them that both must be more or less at fault, and will advise them no longer to quarrel.
>
> (Parel, 2009: 57)

There seems to have been a close connection between Gandhian *ahimsa* and the moral dispositions involved in forgiving and forgetting. The intimate connection between the last two dispositions of character might become clearer if one asks oneself if it is possible to experience complete forgiveness towards anyone who has injured oneself (or one's own people) in the past without being able to forget that injury. If one is truly to forgive another it seems possible to argue that no mark of the past injury *qua* injury can remain in one's memory.

Perhaps it was this idea of working through the memory of past injuries till they had been completely forgotten – as if they had never happened – that had led Gandhi to rethink the meaning of 'history'. In this context it is important to recall the discussion in Chapter XVII of the *Hind Swaraj* on the difference between the term 'history' and it's Gujarati equivalent '*itihaas*'. Gandhi had argued that the sense of '*itihaas*' is '(i)t so happened' (Ibid, 87). Bringing out the difference between '*itihaas*' and 'history', Gandhi wrote that in contrast to '*itihaas*' the term 'history' was

> a record of the wars of the world. . . . How kings played, how they became enemies of one another, and how they murdered one another is found accurately recorded in history.
>
> (Ibid)

Gandhi explained that history was conceived as a discipline providing 'copious evidence' (Ibid) about the 'doings of kings and emperors' (Ibid). As such, the history of a people became the means to keep the memory of all past feuds vivid and alive by meticulously recording them. Having a sense of one's

102 *Bindu Puri*

history as a distinct people had come to mean that a people did not forget great kingdoms, wars and enmities. Gandhi wrote:

> So there is a proverb among Englishmen that a nation which has no history, that is, no wars, is a happy nation.
>
> (Ibid)

Gandhi suggested that one could think differently about the past and one's relationship to it as a people if the past was conceived as '*itihaas*' or 'it so happened'. One can perhaps reinterpret Gandhi's position if one considers the significance of the difference between the meanings of the two terms 'history' and '*itihaas*'. It seems possible to understand why Gandhi should have argued that a discipline conceived in terms of 'it so happened' would have conceptual space for the small narratives that would not provide 'historical evidence' but evidence of 'the force of truth or love' (Ibid) from 'the story of the universe' (Ibid). Such a discipline (quite unlike the discipline with which we are familiar as history) could incorporate the smaller narratives that would for instance tell how 'brothers quarrel' and then later on 'begin to live in peace' (Ibid, 88).

One can connect the Gandhian distinction between history and *itihaas* with Gandhi's emphasis on the connection between developing an *ahimsanat*/non-violent disposition and the ability to forget. Perhaps Gandhi's difficulties with thinking about the past as a meticulous record of the reign of kings, great wars and feuds was that such a way of thinking about the past commits a people to remembering injuries inflicted in the past. This means that memories of past animosities play a constitutive role in a person or a group's responses to different 'others' in the present. Perhaps Gandhi made the argument about the difference between the terms 'history' and '*itihaaas*' to emphasize the connection between *ahimsa*/soul force and forgetting. Quite aptly, the chapter in *Hind Swaraj* in which Gandhi made this argument was titled 'Passive resistance', and the Gujarati equivalent was '*satyagraha-atmabal*'. Gandhi's argument in this chapter was an attempt to suggest that the ability to forget animosities and wrongs done in the past was essential to develop the moral disposition to forgive and be non-violent towards those with whom one had disagreed in the past.

Before concluding this discussion on Gandhian *ahimsa*, it is important to take note of a third virtue that Gandhi often invoked in connection with an *ahimsanat* disposition:

> So long as man does not of his own free put himself last among his fellow creatures, there is no salvation for him. Ahimsa is the farthest limit of humility.
>
> (Prabhu and Rao, 2007: 5)

It is significant to note that the Gandhian conception of the good human life involved the virtue of humility understood as an individual's progress towards

Negotiating differences in a Gandhian way 103

complete egoless-ness. Interestingly Gandhi connected a progressively ego-less good human life with the end or goal of true individual freedom/*swaraj*. In this connection it is important to note that Gandhi conceived of *swaraj* in two senses both as 'self-rule' and as 'home rule'. As the primary meaning of freedom individual self-rule implied a state of the rule of the ego driven self by the higher moral impulses. For Gandhi individual freedom was a state of moral self-rule, which meant that individual egoistic impulses had lost the power to enslave the self. Humility was important to the discipline of becoming free from an over-assertive sense of self. Gandhi had himself made these connections. For instance, while explaining individual freedom in *Hind Swaraj*, he had argued that: 'To observe morality is to attain mastery over our mind and passions' (Gandhi in Parel, 2009: 65).

At another place he said:

> Let us now examine the root of *ahimsa*. It is utter-most selflessness. Selflessness means complete freedom from a regard for one's body.
> (Bose, 1948: 155)

It is interesting to note here that in his *Autobiography* in 1928, Gandhi had recorded that Sir Gurudas Benerji had suggested that humility be added to the list of vows recommended for those living at the *Satyagraha Ashram*. Gandhi commented that though he had been tempted to agree at the time, he refrained from including humility in the list as he 'feared humility would cease to be humility the moment it became a matter of a vow. The true connotation of humility is self-effacement' (Gandhi, *eCWMG* 44: 385). It seems fairly clear that Gandhian non-violence involved the cultivation of a moral disposition involving such self-effacement as well as the practise of compassion, fearlessness, the ability to forget and love for differing 'others'. However, before closing the discussion on *ahimsa* in Gandhi, it is important to remember that Gandhian *ahimsa* cannot be understood without appreciating it as being continuous with truth. This then takes me into the next section of the chapter.

Ahimsa and *satya*

Gandhi had often argued that to arrive at truth it was necessary to meet opposing viewpoints and opposing persons with *ahimsa*. He had emphasised that it was simply not possible to arrive at truth without humility, that is, without overcoming the obstructions caused by one's ego-driven presuppositions. Consequently, the only path to truth in a Gandhian life was through negotiating the otherness of the 'other' and what one saw as the truth-untruths of 'others' with humility and love, i.e., with *ahimsa*. However, this did not mean that Gandhi recommended that when faced with hostility one ought to give up the truth as one saw it. Rather it meant that the path to truth involved suffering in oneself/*tapasya* for the sake of arriving at truth as

104   *Bindu Puri*

opposed to destroying what one saw as the truth-untruths in the possession of others. It was in such a sense that Gandhi spoke of truth and non-violence as inseparably related:

> without ahimsa it is not possible to find truth. Ahimsa and truth are so intertwined that it is practically impossible to disentangle and separate them. They are like the two sides of a coin, or rather of a smooth metallic disc. Who can say which is the obverse, and which is the reverse?
> (Gandhi, *From Yeravda Mandir* in Narayan, 1968, Vol. IV: 219)

As Gandhi so often reiterated, *ahimsa* was the means and truth the end of the good human life. However, since means and end were convertible terms in his understanding of a good life, the relationship between truth and non-violence was constitutive rather than instrumental. One can get a sense of why Gandhi made this connection only once we look more closely at what is involved in Gandhian *ahimsa*. In the words of Gandhi himself:

> This is the path of ahimsa. It may entail continuous suffering and the cultivating of endless patience. . . . Thus step by step we learn to make friends with all the world; we realize the greatness of God – of Truth. Our peace of mind increases in spite of suffering; we become braver and more enterprising. . . . Our pride melts away and we become humble. Our worldly attachments diminish, and the evil within us diminishes from day to day.
>
> (Ibid, 217–218)

The necessary connection between truth and Gandhian *ahimsa* – understood as humility and developing a friendship with all others – can perhaps be better understood if we reflect on the idea that seeing things from within one's own powerfully egocentric perspectives often prevents one from coming close to truth. Often predominantly ego-directed perceptions prevent one from seeing how things really are in the world independently of how we may want to see them. One way in which one might be able to philosophically unpack the relationship between non-violence and truth in Gandhi would be simply by reflecting upon the necessity of becoming free of the ego-driven self if one is to arrive at truth. It is important to note in this context that humility as a freedom from egoistic self-preoccupation was at the heart of Gandhi's sense of *ahimsa* understood as meeting hostile 'others' and their differing viewpoints with love and friendship.

Since Gandhian *ahimsa* and truth were two sides of a coin, *ahimsa* was crucial to arriving at the truth for oneself. This meant that one could only get at the truth in a Gandhian framework by meeting difference with humility and deference. This also meant that for Gandhi the path to moral/religious truths could only be negotiated if one treated those who thought differently from oneself as if they were one's own kin. Treating as one's own meant that

Negotiating differences in a Gandhian way   105

one engaged seriously with difference in order to get at the truth of one's own convictions. Responding with *ahimsa* to 'others' was therefore internal to one's own search for truth. This last point is philosophically significant because this argument suggests that if one is to get at truth it is essential to treat the viewpoints of differing 'others' with the same deference that one feels for one's own beliefs. This implies that one can make a case for treating the views of others with respect and deference without bringing in reasons that are extraneous/external to one's own search for truth. The history of liberalism is replete with arguments to support the recommendation to respect the views of others by reasons external to one's own search for the truth – for instance, that one should defer to the views of others in the interest of creating a reasonably stable and just society. Or again that one should at the very least tolerate the views of opposing others in the interest of peace as a modus vivendi or a truce between opposing positions. The Gandhian connection between truth and *ahimsa* constructs an argument where the route to treating the viewpoints of differing others with deference is internal to an individual's own search for the truth. According to Gandhi, an individual simply cannot get to the truth without *ahimsa*.

Another important philosophical implication of the Gandhian connection between truth and *ahimsa* was that it was constitutive of an alternative epistemology where *ahimsa* understood as equal deference for all viewpoints became an essential pre-requisite to seeing things as they really were or arriving at truth.

To tolerate or to honour: liberalism and Gandhi

A question that could arise at this point would be to ask whether this Gandhian response to difference implied that Gandhi had been influenced by a liberal position. In other words, one could ask if Gandhi was a liberal recommending that one ought to tolerate different and differing 'others'. One can for instance think here about liberal responses to a central issue posed by the pluralism of the contemporary world – that of living with different and hostile religious 'others'. Liberals have given good philosophical reasons for arguing that one must tolerate those who have different religious beliefs from ourselves. Such arguments have of course been extended, both practically and conceptually, to other sorts of differences between oneself and all 'others' who think about truth in opposing ways.

The philosophical reasons that liberals have offered to accept differences recommend at best 'tolerance' of those who differ from oneself. It is philosophically significant to note that most liberal arguments recommending tolerance proceed from a position of uncertainty and scepticism about truth. One can argue that such scepticism makes liberals inherently limited when dealing with differences in the contemporary world because most of the problems associated with pluralism only arise because people have faith in, rather than uncertainty about, their own beliefs. It seems apparent that

106 *Bindu Puri*

liberal arguments that proceed from a position of uncertainty and scepticism about truth may simply not work for those who have faith in their own convictions about truth.

In this context it might be interesting to explore liberal arguments about tolerance made by Mill and Locke as a case in point. Mill makes a meta-inductive argument for tolerance in *On Liberty*. He recommends tolerance on the grounds that people know that they can be wrong and that they are not infallible (Mill, 2006: 24). Mill argues here that even if people have an unshakeable faith in the truth of their own convictions they can still tolerate 'others' who disagree with them because they recognise the value of diversity to the search for the truth. However, this might not work; indeed has often not worked for those who confront conflicting 'others' in the contemporary world for a number of reasons. First, one should note that conflicts arise precisely because people believe and have absolute faith in the truth of their own convictions. Such faith often implies that the faithful are not open to thinking that it is because they might be mistaken that they should toler-ate the opposing beliefs of those with whom they are in conflict. Second, such people certainly might not have a prior and overriding commitment to a comprehensive liberalism that values autonomy and diversity above the truths of their moral religious and cultural convictions.

Besides the fact that tolerance proceeding from a scepticism about the possibility of arriving at truth might not work in the contemporary world, there is also the possibility that liberal tolerance might not be enough. Tol-erance may simply not be adequate when it comes to confronting contem-porary pluralism because the chief characteristic of such pluralism is that it is premised upon the absolute equality of the opposing viewpoints. While tolerance suggests that the one tolerating assumes a superior position, the absolute equality of opposing viewpoints suggests that each viewpoint com-mands respect rather than mere tolerance. It seems possible to argue then that in the contemporary world one might need to respect rather than merely tolerate those who have beliefs different from one's own.

The liberal position about tolerance is not made substantively stronger by examining Locke's arguments for religious tolerance, which of course can be well extended to tolerance towards other kinds of differences. Locke had made a set of arguments for tolerance that appear to be fairly close to those made by Mill. In the 1667 essay on toleration Locke argued, for instance, that religious beliefs are 'purely speculative opinions' (Locke, 1997: 137). In Locke's view, religious worship 'is a thing wholly between God and' the individual. As such being strictly restricted to the private sphere religious worship 'necessarily produces no action which disturbs the community' (Ibid, 138). According to such an argument, a believer must be tolerant to opposing religious 'others' because religion is not only purely speculative but is also a private affair. Consequently, religious belief is of no consequence to an individual's relations with other people in the public sphere. In another essay written in 1676, Locke discussed the relationship between reason and

Negotiating differences in a Gandhian way 107

revelation. He argued there that faith and revelation can never override the claims of reason for one can never be certain about God's having revealed the truth to us.

> For faith can never convince us of anything that contradicts our knowledge. Because, though faith be founded on the testimony of God (which cannot lie), yet we cannot have an assurance of the truth of it greater than our own knowledge.
>
> (Ibid, 249)

Locke's arguments about religious toleration simply reiterate the liberal point that tolerance is an inevitable outcome of uncertainty and scepticism about the possibility of arriving at truth. The same arguments are extended by liberals to morality, ethnicity, culture or indeed any set of truths that one might come to believe as true because of the accidents of time and place.

Gandhi's position is significantly different from that expressed by liberals like Mill and Locke. For one, he is not speaking about toleration as a way of thinking about difference. On a quite different note, he thinks one should honour rather than tolerate all 'other' ways of thinking about truth. Gandhi often suggests that one should think of the truths that others believe in as if they were one's own. In this context one can gain insights about Gandhi's position by looking at some of the things that he said about conflicting religious truths:

> '*Sahishnuta*' is a translation of the English word 'tolerance'. I did not like that word. . . . Kaka Saheb, too, did not like that word. He suggested 'Respect for all religions'. I didn't like that phrase either. Tolerance may imply a gratuitous assumption of the inferiority of other faiths to one's own, and respect suggests a sense of patronizing.
>
> (Gandhi, *eCWMG*, Vol. 50: 78)

Speaking in the context of religious pluralism Gandhi had recommended that rather than speaking about tolerance or respect one should express an equimindedness in learning to 'honour' other religions as 'one's own'. He used the metaphor of kinship to bring out this *samabhava*/equimindedness:

> I have no other wish in this world, but to find light, joy and peace through Hinduism . . . it has enabled me to treat other religions on a footing of absolute equality and their followers even as my blood brothers and sisters.
>
> (Gandhi, *eCWMG*, Vol. 59: 137)

> I, who believe in the absolute equality of the great religions of the world from my early days have learnt to honour other religions as my own.
>
> (Gandhi, *eCWMG*, Vol. 62: 259)

108 *Bindu Puri*

It is interesting that Gandhi should have connected honouring those who differ from oneself with the idea of kinship. As seen in the first section of this chapter, Gandhi had argued that non-violence involved treating those who are hostile to one as one would treat one's own family members. To honour opposing others and conflicting beliefs as one would one's own implies an attitude of sameness and more importantly the acceptance of *samata* or the status of the absolute equality of conflicting beliefs and persons. This is far more exacting than both tolerance and respect. This then is the central point of difference between Gandhi's response to what appeared as the truth-untruths of others and the tolerance recommended by liberals. To tolerate others could suggest the assumption of a superior position. In contrast, the Gandhian idea that one should treat the truths believed in by others like one would one's own implies the attitude of absolute equality while accepting absolute difference. A second way in which Gandhi differed from the liberals was in recommending that different 'others' ought to be honoured. One can argue that honouring opposing others cannot come from a position of equal uncertainty/scepticism about all truth claims but only from the conviction that all those who differ from each other are seeking absolute truth. Gandhi often spoke of truth as God famously changing from 'God is Truth' (Prabhu and Rao, 2007: 51) to 'Truth is God' (Ibid). This equation of truth with God makes it clear that Gandhi was not sceptical about the possibility of arriving at truth. His recommendation to honour all viewpoints then was clearly not based on a liberal-like scepticism about truth claims.

This last point of difference between Gandhi and the liberals has an important bearing on a point with which I started this chapter. I started with the point that Gandhi's response to difference can be a powerful alternative to both liberal tolerance and non-liberal conflict as alternative ways of responding to differing 'others' in the contemporary world. The appeal of the Gandhian response as a third way of responding to difference arises from the fact that Gandhi's way could be acceptable to the faithful and to those who devoutly believe in their own religious moral or cultural truths. This is because Gandhi does not base his arguments recommending deference to all opposing viewpoints on a scepticism about all truth claims. His position on plurality and diversity of truth claims proceeds from the standpoint of the faithful and the devout rather than from that of the sceptic. His position can therefore appeal to the devout as providing good reasons for responding to 'others' with deference while having faith in their own truths. In a Gandhian framework, indeed (as noted in the second section) *ahimsa* is the only means to truth. Consequently, on this view a believer's own progress towards truth cannot proceed without honouring and engaging with the views of those who differ from herself.

Conclusion

This chapter has argued that the contemporary relevance of the Gandhian legacy can be best located in Gandhi's conception of *ahimsa*. Gandhian *ahimsa* is much more than non-injury and involves a host of moral dispositions like compassion, the gift of fearlessness, love and the ability to forget and forgive. The chapter has argued that Gandhian *ahimsa* provides a conceptual resource for rethinking the manner in which one ought to respond to difference in the contemporary world. This presents an alternative to liberal tolerance as the best way of negotiating with difference. One can then conclude this chapter with the thought that the Gandhian argument might provide us with the best reasons for honouring difference in the contemporary plural world.

Notes

1 Gandhi used the word *swabhava* in the sense of man's innermost nature.
2 '*Ahimsa* and *satya*' can be translated as 'non-violence and truth'.

References

Bose, N. K. (ed.). 1948. *Selections from Gandhi* (Ahmedabad: The Navajivan Trust).
Gandhi, Mahatma K. 1968. *From Yeravda Mandir*, in Shriman Narayan (ed.), *The Selected Works of Mahatma Gandhi*, Vol. 4, pp. 211–260 (Ahmedabad: Navajivan Trust).
Gandhi, Mahatma K., *Collected Works of Mahatma Gandhi*, Vol. 1–98, *electronic edition (eCWMG)*, New Delhi: Ministry of Information and Broadcasting, GoI. Accessible online at http://gandhiserve.org/cwmg/cwmg.html.
Locke, John. 1997. *Locke: Political Essays*, edited by Mark Goldie (Cambridge: Cambridge University Press).
Mill, John Stuart. 2006. *On Liberty and Subjection of Women*, edited by Alan Ryan (London: Penguin Classic).
Murti, V. V. Ramana (ed.). 1970. *Gandhi Essential Writings* (New Delhi: Gandhi Peace Foundation).
Parel, Anthony (ed.). 2009. *Hind Swaraj and Other Writings* (New Delhi: Cambridge University Press).
Prabhu, R. K. and Rao, U. R. (eds.). 2007. *The Mind of Mahatma Gandhi* (Ahmedabad: Navajivan Publishing House).

Index

abhaydaan 99–100
aesthetic judgment 8
aesthetic perception 8
ahimsa 4, 8, 10, 12–13, 36, 42, 90, 97,
98, 101, 102, 108, 109; and love 99;
and passive resistance 102; and *satya*
103–105
ahimsa-swabhava 98
Ahmad, Imtiaz 55
Ali, Ameer 61
Ali, M. Mohamed 19
Ambedkar, B. R. 3, 40, 41, 43, 47, 48,
49; *The Annihilation of Caste* 40;
approach to Indian society 45–46;
approach to the economy 44; on
education 42; political stance 43–44
Andrews, C. F. 18–19, 23
appetitive instinct 86–87
Arendt, H. 86
atman 29
atomism 86–87

Bakhtiyar, Shaykh Qutbad-din 6
Banerjee, Prathama 57
baqua 6
Basu, Jyoti 36
Bernstein, Richard 72
Bhagvadgita 36, 42
Bhramcharya experiments 65–66, 67
Bihar earthquake, as 'divine
punishment' 73–75, 76–78
Bilgrami, Akeel 59
Bonney, Charles 36
Brahmanism 49
Buddhism 43, 49

caste 2, 40, 46, 47, 60; and Muslims
60–61; untouchability 3, 43, 44, 48
Ching, Julia 22

Christianity 5–6, 13, 19, 23;
secularism 23
civilization 90
climate change 2
colonialism 40, 47, 55, 56, 73; neo- 72
communalism 55
community 77, 78, 79
compassion 99, 100, 103
confessional study of religion 23–24
conflict 106; with 'others' 97; religious
27; social 46–47, 48
consumerism 4, 93
conversion 2, 18, 19, 20; external 19;
Gandhian 23
craze for machinery 88, 90, 91
cultures 72, 73, 90; and language 11

Dalits 10, 40, 50–51n9
daya 99, 100
deception 10
Descartes, Rene 85, 95n1
Dewey, John 46
diversity 11, 108
'divine punishment' argument 79–80,
81; Gandhian 73–75; Kantian 75–78
dogma 36; and morality 20

Eastern religions 22, 23
economics: Ambedkar's approach 44;
Gandhian 3–4, 91–94
education 23–25, 41, 46; *Nai Talim* 42
ego 7, 8, 103
empathy 100
Engineer, Ashgar Ali 55
Enlightenment, the 73, 74–75, 75, 80,
85; *see also* Kant, Immanuel
equality 3, 42, 45, 64, 93, 107; gender
41; *samata* 108
ethics 92; Gandhian economics 3–4

Index 111

'experiments with truth' 9
external conversion 18, 19; Gandhi on 19
'eye of faith' 43

faith 3, 23, 38n3, 105, 106; 'eye of' 43; 'living' 75, 79, 80; rational 75–76, 77, 78, 79, 80; and revelation 106–107; *see also* religion(s); spirituality
fana 6
fanaticism 2
farj 98
fasts, of Gandhi 9
fearlessness 99–100, 101, 103
'fellowship of religions' 2, 15
feminism 10, 11
forgetfulness 6, 101
forgiveness 101
freedom 3, 10, 48, 75, 88; individual 103; religious 2; *see also* religious freedom

Gandhi, Mahatma 2, 3, 5, 9, 11, 13, 17, 18, 20, 27, 35, 36, 37, 40, 41, 42, 47, 48, 49, 56, 63, 72, 73, 85, 86, 89, 101; and Ambedkar 3; approach to history 42; approach to Indian society 45–46; approach to the economy 44; *Autobiography* 103; *Bhramcharya* experiments 65–66, 67; 'divine punishment' argument 73–75, 78–80, 81; economic vision 91–94; education 82n4; on external conversion 19; fasts 9; *Hind Swaraj* 1, 3, 27, 57–58, 59, 63–64, 98, 99, 101, 103; on Hinduism 14, 31; on history 101–102; how to read 57; interpretation of modernity 86–87; on invention 91; legacy of 97; and liberalism 105–108; Muslim appeasement 55; on Muslims 58, 66–67; *My Experiments with Truth* 1; philosophy of 59; politics of 43–44; on the *Quran* 64–65; relativist position on religion 12–13; on religion 27–28, 30, 31, 32; *satyagraha* 35; on the study of religion 24–25
gender equality 41; Muslim women 69–70n12
globalisation 94
God 5, 15, 21, 23, 27–28, 78, 108; *baqua* 6; conversion 2; and 'divine punishment' 73–75, 76–78; and truth 2; *see also* self-knowledge
Golwalkar, M. S. 55
good human life 100, 102, 103, 104

Hasan, Mushirul 55
Heidegger, Martin 85, 86, 87, 95n3
himsa 15
Hinduism 6, 7, 11–12, 13, 24, 25, 29, 30, 40, 43, 47, 49; *atman* 29; *Bhagvadgita* 36; conflict with Islam 33–34, 35, 37, 43–44, 56, 58, 60, 63–65; Gandhi on 14, 31, 59; *maya* 29; *mukti* 29; *samsara* 10; untouchability 43; *see also ahimsa*; religious conflict
history: Ambedkar on 42; Gandhi on 63–64, 101–102; Islamic 61–62; and '*itihaas*' 101–102
human rights 2
humility 9, 102, 103

identity 10, 14; of Muslims 68; religious 21–22, 23
India 10, 15, 19, 72; comparing Ambedkar and Gandhi's approach to society 45–46; cultures 11; homogeneity of Muslims 55–56, 61–62, 68; Khilafat movement 55, 69n3; Partition 2; religious conflict in 12; villages 48–49
individualism 86–87, 88
industrialisation 93
inequality 1
instinctive feeling 80, 81
internal conversion 18, 19
inventions 90–91
Iqbal: *Jawab-e-Shikwa* 62; *Shikwa* 61–62
Islam 3, 13, 19, 23, 32, 33; conflict with Hinduism 33–34, 35, 37, 43–44, 56, 58, 60, 63–65; history of imperialism 63; Khilafat movement 69n3; and morality 68; *umma* 67; *see also Quran*; religious conflict
'*itihaas*' 101, 102

Jinnah, Muhammed Ali 3, 33, 35; on religion 33–34
Jones, Richard 89
Judaism 23
justice 12–13, 64; universal 65

112   Index

Kant, Immanuel 3, 8, 73; and the 'divine punishment' argument 75–78, 79, 81; *Religion within the Boundaries of Mere Reason* 76
Khadi 43, 45, 94
Khilafat movement 55, 69n3
kinship 98, 99, 107, 108
knowledge 76; scientific 41, 74–75; self- 5, 6, 7, 9, 10, 42; sensory 6; of truth 5

language 7; and culture 11
liberalism, and Gandhi 105–108
liberation 37
'living faith' 75, 79, 80
Locke, John 106, 107
love, and *ahimsa* 99

Madan, T. N. 55
madrasa 23–24
Mahadevan, T.M.P. 23
Manusmriti 42
Marcuse, H. 86
'martial races' 60
mass production 93
materialism 93
maya 29
Mcghee, Michael 8
meditation 5–6, 9
Mehta, Raychandbhai 100; *Mokshamala* 99
Michaels, Axel, *Hinduism: Past and Present* 21
Mill, John Stuart, *On Liberty* 106
Minault, Gail 55
mission 18
modernity 72, 86, 87, 88, 95; and individualism 86–87; and morality 88; technological reductionism 88–91; and technology 85; *see also* technology
'modern turn' 3, 47, 48
morality 2, 3, 7, 8, 23, 88, 90; and 'divine punishment' 74–75, 76–78, 79–81; and dogma 20; and feminism 10–11; Islamic 68; and self-education 8; and self-knowledge 7; and truth 9
Mughal 61
Mujeeb, Mohammed 55
mukti 29
music, *quwwal* 6
Muslims 3, 19, 68; in the caste system 61; Gandhi on 58, 59; Gandhi's appeasement of 55; homogeneity of 55–56, 61, 62, 68; Khilafat

movement 55, 69n3; 'martial races' 60; women 69–70n12; *see also* Islam; religious conflict
mysticism 2, 9; *see also* superstition

Nai Talim 42
Narvane, V. S. 37
natural disasters, as 'divine punishment' 73–75, 76–78, 79–81
negative secularism 23
neo-colonialism 72
neutral secularism 23
Nietzsche, Friedrich 85, 95n2
Nigam, Aditya 57
nihilism 85
non-confessional study of religion 24
non-positivism 41
non-violence 8–9, 37, 44, 48, 58, 108; *see also ahimsa*; religious conflict

'others' 4, 10, 97, 98, 100, 106; empathetic identification with 100; forgiving 101

Panchayat Raj 48
Pandey, Rakesh 57
Partition of India 2, 56
passive resistance 102
Pathan 61
philosophy 15, 35, 85; of Gandhi 59; Indian thought 72; non-positivism 41; reductionism 89; technological reductionism 88–91, 95; *see also* Kant, Immanuel
plurality of religions 11–15
political action 46
politics: of Ambedkar 43–44; feminism 10–11; of Gandhi 43–44; of self-knowledge 10–11; and violence 66; *see also satyagraha*
Poona Pact 40
positive secularism 23
practical life 1
prayer 6
progress 86; technological reductionism 88–91
proselytization *see* external conversion

Quran 3, 24, 58, 63, 68; Gandhi's reading of 64–65
quwwal 6

rational faith 75–77, 78, 79, 80
reductionism, technological 88–91, 95
relativist position on religion 12–13

Index   113

religion(s) 2, 5, 9, 15, 27, 38n2, 41, 42–43, 99, 100, 107; Christianity 5–6, 19, 23; conclusiveness of 20; confessional study of 23–24; and conflict 27; conversion 2, 18, 19, 20; Eastern 22, 23; exclusiveness of 20–21, 29, 30, 31, 32; fellowship of 15; Gandhi on 27–28, 30, 31, 32; Hinduism 6, 7, 11–12; Islam 3, 23, 32, 33; Jinnah on 35; mission 18; non-confessional study of 24; phenomenological study of 24–25; plurality of 11–15; principle of singular adherence 29; relativist position on 12–13; rituals 31; Sufism 6; temporal aspects 14; Western 21; world 24; *see also* 'divine punishment' argument; religious conflict; religious freedom; religious identity

religious conflict 27, 28–29, 35, 38, 46–47, 56, 58; Gandhi and Jinnah 33; Hindu-Islam 34–36, 37, 43–44, 60, 63–65

religious freedom 2, 17, 18, 19, 20; and conversion 23; and education 23–25; Gandhian 20–21; and religious identity 21–22, 23; and secularism 23; *see also* Universal Declaration of Human Rights

religious identity 21–22, 23
rituals 31
Roy, Arundhati 40
Roy, M. N. 36

samata 108
samsara 6, 7, 10
sarvodaya 37, 91, 92, 94
satya, and *ahimsa* 103–105; *see also* truth
satyagraha 4, 10, 35, 36, 37, 46, 94, 102; *see also* truth
science 41
sectarianism 27
secularism 21, 23; Gandhian 23
self, the 6
self-disclosure 86–87
self-discovery 8
self-education 8
self-knowledge 2, 5, 6, 9, 10, 42; and morality 7; politics of 10–11
self-perfection 42
seminary 23–24
sensory knowledge 6

Sheikhs 61
social endosmosis 46
Soskice, Janet Martin, 'Love and Attention' 5–6
soul, the 86, 87; *atman* 29
spirituality 5–6, 6, 7, 9, 10, 11, 12–13, 23, 86, 92; and the 'divine punishment' argument 78–79; and self-knowledge 10; and truth 11; *see also* 'divine punishment' argument; morality; religion(s)
sthitaprajna 6
Strachey, John, *India* 60, 61
Sufism 6; *baqua* 6; *fana* 6
superstition 3, 72, 76–77, 78, 79
swabhava 98
swadeshi 91, 92, 94
swadharma 1
swaraj 3, 9, 37, 41, 44, 45, 46, 47, 48, 49, 91, 92, 103
Syed 61

Tagore, Rabindranath 3, 73, 74–75
tapasya 103–104
Taylor, Charles 86–87
technological reductionism 88–91, 95
technology 3, 85, 86, 92; craze for machinery 88, 90–91, 93; Gandhian economics 91–94; inventions 90–91; mass production 93; and modernity 87, 88
temporal aspects of religion 14
tolerance 4, 97, 98, 105, 106, 107
truth 1, 4, 5, 14, 31, 79, 103–104, 106, 107, 108; 'experiments with' 9; and God 2; and spirituality 11

Universal Declaration of Human Rights, Article 18 17–18
untouchability 3, 43, 44, 46, 47, 48

varna system 40
villages 48–49
violence 66
virtues 7

Western religions 21
Wittgenstein, Ludwig, *Culture and Value* 8
world religions 24

yeshiva 23–24
yuga dharma 1

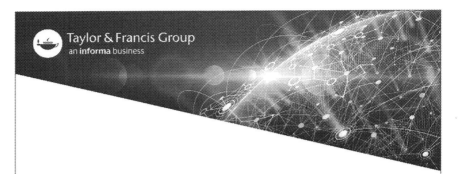

Printed in the United States
by Baker & Taylor Publisher Services